Anti-Bum Shield

YOUR ARMOR AGAINST POVERTY

or How the World of Finance Really Works

Davy Mairon

© 2024 by Davy Mairon

ISBN: 9798322418757

All rights reserved. No part of this book may be reproduced or used in any form or by any means, electronic or mechanical, including photocopying, recording, or by any information storage and retrieval system, without permission in writing from the publisher, except for brief quotations embodied in critical articles and reviews.

Contact the Author:

Join the Telegram Group to engage with the author and other readers, discuss the book's themes, and access exclusive content and resources.

Visit https://t.me/+xFYBw5gvliIyYjEy to become a part of our community.

"I believe that if you show people the problems and you show them the solutions, they will be moved to act." - Bill Gates

Contents

INTRODUCTION 3
READING RECOMMENDATIONS 6
CHAPTER 1: "ANTI-BUM SHIELD". DEFINITION OF
SALES. PACKAGING 8
    KEY IDEAS OF CHAPTER ONE 17
CHAPTER 2: HOW VALUE IS DETERMINED 20
    KEY IDEAS OF CHAPTER TWO 32
CHAPTER 3: WHAT IS IMPORTANT FOR A WEALTHY
PERSON? 34
    KEY IDEAS OF CHAPTER THREE 45
CHAPTER 4: MONETARY RELATIONSHIPS AND
BENEFITS 47
    KEY IDEAS OF CHAPTER FOUR 58
CHAPTER 5: "MONEY PLACE" AND OPPORTUNITIES 60
    KEY IDEAS OF CHAPTER FIVE 70
CHAPTER 6: SENSING PEOPLE. TACTFULNESS 72
    KEY IDEAS OF CHAPTER SIX 80
CHAPTER 7: BENEFIT DOES NOT EQUAL MONEY 82
    KEY IDEAS OF CHAPTER SEVEN 96
CHAPTER 8: BUSINESS IS A BLUFF 98
    KEY IDEAS OF CHAPTER EIGHT 108
CHAPTER 9: HOW TO CREATE BELIEF THAT WHAT
YOU OFFER IS WORTH A LOT? 110
    KEY IDEAS OF CHAPTER NINE 116
CHAPTER 10: TO SELL, YOU MUST FEEL ENTITLED 118

KEY IDEAS OF CHAPTER TEN 130
CHAPTER 11: MIGHT IS RIGHT **132**
    KEY IDEAS OF CHAPTER ELEVEN 141
CHAPTER 12: THE TWO TYPES OF PROBLEMS **143**
    KEY IDEAS OF CHAPTER TWELVE 153
APPENDIX 155
NOTES 157

Introduction

In a society where achieving financial prosperity can often feel unattainable, it is simple to experience a sense of confusion and disorientation. We all desire to enhance our lives, however, the journey towards reaching our objectives can be ambiguous. That's the reason I have dedicated numerous hours exploring for the perfect concept to write a book that would assist individuals in comprehending the intricate world and potentially improving their lives.

After much contemplation, I stumbled upon Arsen Markaryan's private channel stream, and it was like a lightbulb went off in my head. Arsen, an Armenian dollar millionaire and owner of one of the largest private channels on Telegram, is renowned for delivering on his promises and helping his students achieve remarkable results. His advice, rooted in personal experience, cuts through the noise and provides the essential knowledge needed to shift your perspective and create lasting change.

This book is designed for anyone who wants to see the world through a different lens. Whether you're just starting out in business, looking to improve your existing venture, or find yourself at a crossroads, unsure of how to move forward, this book is for you. It's a must-read for those curious about the inner workings of the human-created financial mechanism that drives our world.

Inside these pages, you won't find a lot of fluff or filler. Instead of that, you will come across actual instances from life and important perspectives, which will aid in grasping the psychology behind the realm of money. You will understand the reasons why individuals choose to purchase from one person over another and what drives their purchasing decisions initially. You will learn the reasons why YOU deserve to $5000 for a gym training sessions with a millionaire and how to build the self-assurance to do it.

Although you may be content with your current results, this book will increase your knowledge of the financial world and offer tools to further improve your success. Once you complete reading, you will possess the necessary knowledge and mindset for changing yourself and your financial future.

However, it's important to note that I never encourage anyone to blindly follow the examples provided in this book. To truly benefit from the insights within, you must be willing to think critically and process the information for yourself. You need to be ready to accept new ideas and challenge your existing beliefs. Only then can you fully grasp the power of the knowledge presented and apply it effectively to your own life.

So, if you're an entrepreneur, a business owner, or just someone who wants to gain a deeper understanding of finance and human psychology, this book is one of the best choices for you. Prepare to explore a realm of enlightening perspectives and useful recommendations that will forever alter your perceptions of wealth and success.

READING RECOMMENDATIONS

If you want to truly benefit from this book, you must be prepared to confront some harsh realities. I am not here to treat you with excessive care or guide you through every step. I'm here to offer you genuine advice that lead you to make significant improvements in your life.

Some of you may be thinking, "This writing style is too harsh for my taste." Sorry, bad luck, sweetie. This book is not suitable for those who are easily scared. It is for individuals who are prepared to seize control of their own lives and make things happen. If you are unable to withstand some harsh criticism, perhaps this book is not suitable for you.

It's crucial to understand that people only truly absorb information when they're ready for it. Think back to a time when someone offered you advice, and you initially dismissed it, only to later realize the wisdom in their words. To fully benefit from this book, prepare yourself to accept information that could potentially challenge your existing views on the world.

If you're still present, that means you possess the necessary qualities. Therefore, make sure to carefully go through every chapter as if your life is at stake. Don't just glance over the pages and believe you understand everything. Truly delve into your thoughts and confront the tough inquiries.

I included those questions at the conclusion of every chapter with intention - they serve a purpose beyond mere decoration.

To aid in your understanding and personal growth, each chapter concludes with key ideas and thought-provoking questions. These questions are designed to help you identify areas for improvement and pinpoint exactly what needs to change in your life.

If you feel like giving up, please turn to the appendix at the end of the book before making any decisions. I have included some crucial content in it, and I assure you it will provide you with the motivation you need to continue.

Don't forget, this book is your key to a superior existence. However, it won't happen through magic. You must be prepared to work hard and confront difficult truths about yourself and your surroundings. If you are prepared to take that step, I guarantee that the benefits will make it worthwhile.

Chapter 1: "Anti-Bum Shield". Definition of sales. Packaging

Anti-Bum Shield

Let's be real - a lot of people think selling is some sleazy, manipulative thing reserved for con artists and used car dealers. They picture slick-haired salesmen in cheap suits pestering people into buying junk they don't need.

But here's the truth: When done right, selling is simply facilitating a mutually beneficial exchange. The buyer gets something valuable that improves their life, and the seller gets fairly compensated for providing that value. Simple as that. No trickery required.

The problem is, too many businesses, especially small ones and startups, treat selling as an unfortunate chore. They timidly tiptoe around it, almost embarrassed to be "one of those salespeople." News flash - selling is the lifeblood of any business! You either get good at ethically persuading people to buy, or your venture dies. Period.

Besides, like it or not, we're all in sales every single day. Convincing your kid to eat their veggies? Sales. Getting buy-in for your ideas at work? Sales. Swiping right and crafting the perfect Tinder message? Sales! Anytime you attempt to get someone to take a desired action, you're flexing your persuasion muscles. Might as well build those muscles intentionally so you can win in business and in life.

Now, I know what you might be thinking: "Sure, but my widget is nothing special. How can I compete with cheaper options?" Enter the magic of packaging, my friend. I'm not talking about slapping your logo on a cardboard box - I mean strategically showcasing your offer in a way that elevates its perceived value.

Quick example. Let's say you're shopping for a birthday gift. On a table, there's a plain ballpoint pen, naked as the day it was manufactured. Right next to it is an identical pen, but this one is ensconced in a gorgeous rosewood box with gold embossed lettering spelling out "Executive Pen Set." Which one would you naturally grab for your classy uncle? The packaged one! Even though the core product is the same, the upscale packaging creates an aura of specialness and value.

This applies to services too. If you're an accountant, you're not just "doing taxes" - you're providing a comprehensive financial optimization experience. See how that positioning creates a different flavor than simply being a numbers grunt?

Anti-Bum Shield

Here's the key: With the right packaging, price becomes a mere triviality. If you can effectively communicate the value of your offer - through your marketing, sales process, branding, the whole shebang - then the sticker price is like a tiny bug on the windshield of your persuasion racecar. Irrelevant.

Think about trendy designer jeans. Why are people willing to pay $200+ for denim that likely cost $10 to manufacture? Because the brands have masterfully packaged an intangible aura of prestige, status, and exclusivity around their products. The price is no longer about the tangible materials, it's about buying entrance into an aspirational experience.

Now, this doesn't mean you should just make up sparkly nonsense about your offerings. The most effective, ethical packaging highlights legitimate value and transforms it into an appealing experience in your prospect's mind.

For example, maybe you sell handmade ceramic mugs. You could just say "Sturdy mug for coffee or tea - $25," but that doesn't really evoke a "take my money!" emotion. Instead, try something like:

"Each of our artisan mugs is a small sculptural masterpiece, lovingly hand-thrown by skilled craftspeople using locally-sourced clay. The organic, one-of-a-kind imperfections in the glaze are a celebration of authentic home goods in an era of mass production. Sipping your morning brew from one of these beauties isn't just a daily ritual - it's a mindful moment of appreciating the luxury of true craftsmanship. Sure, a factory-made mug does the job, but an artisan mug turns the entire experience into a soul-nourishing indulgence."

Boom! See how that takes a basic commodity item - a cup for drinking liquid - and transforms it into a meaningful, almost magical experience? You've just given the buyer a compelling story to justify the price and feel great about their purchase.

Caveat: This packaging only works if it's authentic. If you're just blowing smoke, people will smell the B.S. and bolt. It has to come from a place of genuinely striving to deliver exceptional value and thoughtfully expressing that value.

Masterful packaging alone probably won't sell a turd. But when you combine a legitimately excellent product or service with brilliantly-crafted packaging, you create an offer that's more "HELL YEAH!" than

Anti-Bum Shield

"meh." An offer that makes paying premium prices feel like scoring an amazing deal rather than getting ripped off.

That's Anti-Bum Armor in a nutshell. It's the art of wrapping your offers in an impenetrable layer of value so compelling, it repels bargain hunters and attracts high-quality buyers eager to invest in an exceptional experience.

Too many entrepreneurs and salespeople walk around fully exposed, trying to sell their awesome stuff stark-naked. Then they get hit with a barrage of price objections, lowball offers, and tire-kickers wasting their time. It's demoralizing and destructive to your bottom line.

But when you encase yourself in that Anti-Bum Armor of premium packaging, you deflect those slings and arrows like they're Nerf darts bouncing off a tank. You're no longer nervously hoping prospects will see your value - you're confidently conveying that value with every inch of your persuasion strategy.

This applies across the board - products, services, digital offerings, events, you name it. World-class packaging elevates perceived value so dramatically, price is almost an afterthought. People don't focus on cost when they're enchanted by the promise of a delightful, rewarding experience. In fact, a premium price often amplifies that enchantment by signaling top-tier quality.

Take Apple for instance. They don't just sell tech gadgets - they sell a sleek, chic lifestyle environment. The packaging, from the gleaming storefronts to the artfully minimalist device cases, is all part of creating an irresistible experience that happens to include circuit boards and pixels. A $1000 iPhone isn't just a phone (because c'mon, you could get a decent android for like $200) - it's a status symbol, a portal to a world of gorgeous apps and cutting-edge cred. The packaging and positioning transform it into a statement piece customers can't wait to show off.

Or look at luxury hotels. You're not paying $800 a night for a place to crash - you're paying for a meticulously-curated experience of being treated like royalty. The packaging elements, like decadent bed linens, breathtaking views, and personalized service, all work in harmony to create an opulent mirage that makes the nightly rate seem perfectly reasonable. No one in that penthouse suite is stressing about the price - they're soaking in the grandiosity of an epic experience.

That's the bar you should aspire to with your own packaging. Not misleading flash or fake exclusivity, but a thoughtful, authentic expression of the incredible value you deliver, wrapped in an attention-grabbing experience.

How you actually package your specific offerings depends on your niche and audience. Maybe it's elite-level service, or lavish unboxing moments, or access to an engaged community. The tactics can differ, but the overall strategy is universal: Make your prospect FEEL the unmistakable value of your offer through carefully-constructed packaging that sparks imagination and anticipation.

When you get that dialed in, selling becomes infinitely easier and more profitable. You're no longer pleading with prospects to understand your worth - you're inviting them to step into an aspirational experience that deeply resonates with their wants and beliefs. The price becomes an entry fee they're happy to pay.

So start thinking about your Anti-Bum Armor. How can you take your innately valuable products or services and reframe them as essential ingredients in an extraordinary experience? What elements can you add or accentuate to reinforce that value story? How can you guide prospects to not just intellectually appreciate your offering, but to yearn for the transformation it provides?

Get crystal clear on those packaging points, then make sure every aspect of your marketing and sales process seductively conveys that heightened value. The words you use in your website copy, the visuals in your social content, the nuances in your sales conversations - it all needs to harmonize around that central value-packed experience.

You're not manipulating, you're magnetizing. You're establishing yourself as a premium provider of remarkable experiences, not a cookie-cutter commodity. You're filtering out hagglers so you can serve your true fans at the highest level. And you're doing it all through masterful packaging that dials your perceived value to eleven.

Key Ideas of Chapter One

1. Successful sales strategies focus on creating a situation where both parties feel they are gaining more than they are giving away.

2. The value of a product or service is not solely determined by its inherent qualities but significantly by the perception of its value to the consumer. This perception can be influenced by how the offering is presented or "packaged."

3. Packaging is about thoughtfully showcasing your offer in a way that creates an aspirational experience for buyers.

4. Premium packaging makes price much less important compared to the overall value conveyed.

5. Every aspect of your marketing and sales must reinforce this value-focused packaging. In services and personal interactions, it encompasses the way an offering is communicated, the expectations set, and the overall experience promised to the customer.

Questions for self-development

- Have I ever felt that I received more value than what I paid for? What about the opposite?

- Do I have mental hangups about selling that are holding me back from packaging my offers in the most compelling way possible?

- Am I positioning my products/services as premium, value-packed experiences, or am I just presenting them as basic commodities?

- How can I more strongly showcase the authentic transformation and value my offers provide?

- What elements can I add to my offer packaging to create a "HELL YEAH!" response instead of "meh"?

- Is my current packaging attracting bargain hunters or high-quality, value-seeking buyers? What needs to change?

- How can I infuse my marketing and sales process with the compelling value story of my offers?

Anti-Bum Shield

- What would it look like if I truly believed in the value of what I'm selling? How would that confidence change my packaging?

Chapter 2: How value is determined

Anti-Bum Shield

A harsh reality that most people avoid acknowledging is that value has absolutely nothing to do with objective factors like labor, materials, or production costs. These inputs, while seemingly relevant, are often disregarded by those who determine the value of goods or services.

For proof, think about an iPhone that costs $1,000+. Does the average buyer scrutinize the bill of materials, labor hours, R&D expenses, etc. to evaluate if that price is justified? Of course not. They simply perceive the overall experience and utility as being worth that cost based on their personal situation and Apple's positioned brand value.

As a thought experiment, let's say tomorrow Apple disabled every iPhone across an entire country, rendering them all useless expensive bricks. What would those phones be worth then? Absolutely nothing, despite no change to the underlying manufacturing inputs.

The value dropped to zero because the specific utility and positioned brand relevance that buyers purchased it for disappeared completely based on circumstances. This illustrates how value is purely subjective to each buyer's unique situation, not tethered to objective costs.

Need another example? Think about when you're extremely thirsty and someone has the last cold water bottle. Its inherent value at that desperate moment is exponentially higher than if you were just casually browsing a grocery aisle. The bottle's materials and production costs are identical, but its value fluctuates wildly based on relevance to your precise situation.

You've likely experienced this first-hand through tough negotiations where both sides aggressively bartered to extract maximum value, ignoring shrunken rationales like perceived costs. Each party perceived high value based on their specific circumstances at that moment, and aimed to craft a deal where they got an even better personal outcome through persuasion and gamesmanship. Objective factors were utterly irrelevant.

That's the harsh truth: Something's value is simply what motivated buyers are willing to pay based on their unique situations, not any universal calculation of labor or material inputs. Those inputs may set crude pricing floors, but they don't actually determine value in either direction.

Value is purely in the eye of the beholder based on their immediate needs and perceptions, circumstances, and what they're envisioning the extended ownership experience will provide. It has nothing to do with your costs as the provider. Those are your problem to solve profitably, not the buyer's consideration.

This principle applies to every single product, service, and offer — from iPhones and BMWs to Starbucks coffees and Michelin-starred restaurant experiences to coaching programs and software tools. The objective costs and labor expended are utterly irrelevant to buyers when evaluating primary value. They only care about their individualized perception of subjective worth based on envisioned desire in that moment.

Yet most sellers suffering from broke-minded cognitive biases still default to attaching their pricing to factors like labor hours, complexity of materials, or their own dainty idea of what "seems reasonable." And by doing so, they arbitrarily limit their pricing capabilities solely based on elements buyers don't actually consider.

The savvy move is to detach from those phony, self-imposed constraints and instead diligently study your target buyers' specific situations and motivators. What utility, status, or aspirational outcomes are they truly willing to pay premiums for at that exact window in time? That's where you'll find the real value centers to package premium offers around.

For example, let's say you offer personalized nutrition coaching and custom meal plans. The true value you provide has nothing to do with your own labor hours, expertise development, software costs, or any factors pertaining to your processes. Those are your operational expenses to manage profitably, not value inputs.

The real value centers revolve around reducing your clients' daily stress over meal planning, anxiety about making poor food choices, hassles from grocery shopping/cooking, lost productivity from afternoon energy dips, long-term health downsides from poor diets, status frustrations from not looking/feeling their best, etc. Those are the highly specific outcomes and transformations they'd be willing to pay premium prices for from their in-the-moment pained perspectives.

Anti-Bum Shield

Your objective is to deeply understand those acute value drivers for your specific buyer personas, then package your offers as premium-priced conduits for delivering those desired outcomes and relieving those squeeze points. When you align with what buyers truly crave from their vantage point, your pricing starts detaching from industry practices like service inputs and becomes firmly rooted in the high-value results you're delivering.

For another example, let's say you provide coaching and consulting for entrepreneurs and business owners. You could ignorantly cap your pricing based on typical hourly rates or lowly project budgets in your industry. Or you could discard those external pricing frames and dig into the lucrative value centers your clients actually care about:

- Rapidly implementing systems to reclaim more personal time and freedom from the business

- Achieving a consistent month-over-month revenue run rate through reliability/predictability

- Confidently optimizing operations, cash flow, growth strategies, hiring/firing, etc.

- Amplifying their authority and industry influence for higher premiums and opportunities

- Systemizing the business to minimize crushing workloads and owner reliance

- Income producing assets unlock more passive revenue streams

- Positioning the business to command a potential life-changing exit valuation and multiple later

Those are the emotionally-charged value centers your buyers are desperate to achieve more than any inputs required on your end. If you package offers that convincing aligns with delivering those relevant outcomes in premium value framing, pricing integrity becomes a non-issue because the laser-focused value proposition overshadows it.

You get to circumvent pricing games altogether by extracting the genuine underlying value drivers for your market, then embodying offers that authoritatively pledge those valuable transformations. From that position of being the premium solution to their acute needs, you possess pricing sovereignty to identify the appropriate investment levels based on the lofty outcomes you're enabling.

Master this detached, clinical approach to pinpointing your buyers' truest value perceptions while disregarding

Anti-Bum Shield

your own service inputs, and you eliminate pricing insecurity once and for all. You simply become an objective conduit for delivering the specific valuable outcomes your market craves, and confidently price accordingly with gravitational interstitial pressure.

For far too long, entrepreneurs and businesses have been brainwashed into limited pricing beliefs centered around factors completely irrelevant to actual buyers. They self-cap based on lame platitudes like hourly rates, project formulas, or gooey feelings about what "seems reasonable" to charge based on their personal financial characteristics. It's pricing from a value-neutering scarcity perspective centered on their own story instead of aligning with the valuable transformations their buyers are starving for.

What liberated your pricing policy and self-worth is realizing that your service inputs are meaningless to the buyers evaluating your offers - aside from ensuring you can professionally deliver on promised results, of course. But the factors that actually determine perceived value and willingness to invest are the specific outcomes you package as premium solutions to your target market's acute pain points and aspirations.

For example, buyers don't care if your nutrition coaching program includes 5, 15 or 50 many hours of labor or any specifics on your operational overhead. Those are non-factors to their pricing evaluations. But if you package the program to convincingly solve their biggest headache around healthy meal planning, portions, grocery lists, food prep, etc. in a way that delightfully transforms their dietary consistency, energy levels, body composition, confidence, and quality of life - well then pricing under market rates just looks laughable considering the tremendous value delivered.

The same is true for business coaching/consulting where your expertise hours, administrative complexities or any other service inputs are irrelevant. What matters is your packaging prowess around reducing their deepest fears of revenue inconsistencies, growth stagnation, team mismanagement, lack of personal freedom, inability to confidently execute, minimizing workloads, systemizing for a potential sell, etc.

If you can convincingly portray your program as a comprehensive solution for addressing those urgent entrepreneurial pain points and aspirations, objective input pricing becomes laughably irrelevant. You're no longer aiming to justify hourly rates or project costs - you've firmly established your premium value

Anti-Bum Shield

proposition around delivering highly-specific outcomes they'd pay virtually any amount to achieve.

At that point, your pricing policy stems from the perpetual value your outcomes represent, not trivialities like man-hours or perceived complexity of service deliverables. You're the master solution to their premium value equation, with correlated pricing you control rather than meager rates controlled by external forces.

This is a vastly different paradigm from being an input-based service provider at the mercy of market price ceilings and shrunken self-worth based on skewed value perspectives. When you detach from micromanaged service inputs as determinants of value, suddenly pricing transcends from an exercise in cheap compromises into an extension of the renewable premium transformation buyers crave.

Shed the blind subservience to hourly rates, project formulas, undercharging out of guilt, or other arbitrary value handcuffs. Unmistakably identify your target buyers' utmost relevant value zones where price is no object if anticipated outcomes are convincingly delivered. Build exhaustively premium offers explicitly aligned with gratifying those lofty value obsessions from their starved vantage point.

Then state your pricing as the admission fee for accessing those transformational experiences, not as a puddle of compromised compensation for your inputs. From that astute value perspective where you control the premium narrative through masterful packaging and promise facilitation, pricing is simply the revenue coefficient of your enabled perpetual buyer value, not some subjugated number sitting beneath your expertise worth.

Exit the days of capping your deserved value capture or confidently underpricing from years of financially oppressive brainwashing about input costs, hourly rates, project budgets, or any other upside-limiting pricing policies fueled by external frugal frames instead of definitive premium value facilitation. You're no longer a discount commodity - you're a premium transformation enabler with pricing sovereignty to match.

Let input obsessives grovel, race to the bottom, and cap their ceiling on pricing forever. Your high-road divergence is recognizing those factors as completely irrelevant to the value equation for buyers who only comprehend premium investments through the lens of their specific desired outcomes. As the master conduit for funneling their aspirations into reality through irresistible offer progressions, your justified pricing is simply the permanent expression of your transformative buyer value enablement, not a meager trade of commoditized inputs.

Master aligning your offer packaging to distinct premium value nodes over input rationalizing, and pricing integrity will stem seamlessly from the elite perpetual elevation you authoritatively command in your market's consciousness. You'll chuckle at antiquated pricing strategies centered around shallow input minutiae, and luxuriate in the pricing sovereignty that emerges from being a premium value delivery authority. Claim that liberated pricing plane as your natural ecosystem, and watch your income flourish in tandem with the transformational perpetual value you perpetually create.

Key Ideas of Chapter Two

1. Value is in the eye of the beholder, based on their unique situation, not your costs and inputs.

2. Study your target buyers to identify the outcomes and transformations they value most.

3. Individuals' perceptions of value and their willingness to pay vary significantly based on their economic situations, highlighting the need for tailored approaches in sales and service pricing.

4. Package your offers to directly align with delivering those highly-desired results.

5. Base your pricing on the perpetual value you provide buyers, not your hourly rates or project costs.

6. Claim your pricing authority by being a confident solution to buyers' most pressing needs.

Questions for self-development

- Am I basing my prices on my own internal costs and inputs or on my buyers' value perceptions?

Anti-Bum Shield

- Do I really understand the deepest pain points, aspirations and desired outcomes of my target buyers?

- How can I repackage my offers to more directly address those key value zones for my buyers?

- Am I leaving money on the table by pricing based on my inputs vs. the ongoing results I enable?

- Where am I still stuck in hourly rate or project cost pricing rather than value-based pricing?

- How can I better position and price myself as a premium solution vs. a commodity service provider?

- What would it look like if I fully claimed my pricing authority based on my confidence in the buyer transformations I deliver?

Chapter 3: What is important for a wealthy person?

Anti-Bum Shield

When dealing with affluent buyers, there is one concern that towers over all others: The fear of being ripped off or having their valuable time wasted on an overhyped disappointment.

Think about it this way - if you're wealthy enough to not sweat material costs, what's your biggest scarcest resources? Your time and your peace of mind. You can always make more money, but you can't make more time. And few things are more frustrating than feeling like you've been conned into wasting your limited life force.

That's why the wealthy place such an exorbitant premium on certainty and accountability when they're prospecting any product, service, or investment. They're terrified of being taken for a ride by some overpromising charlatan more interested in extracting a quick buck than actually delivering an exceptional experience.

You've likely encountered this fear in action if you've ever pitched an affluent buyer, investor, or prospect. No matter how thoroughly you laid out the proposition's potential upside, they inevitably started grilling you about "What if it doesn't work out?" or "How can I be assured this isn't just empty hype?"

Those aren't random curveball questions - they're instinctive defenses stemming from that wealthy person's pathological necessity to avoid disappointment and validation of their perpetual battle against grifters trying to prey on their success.

For example, a few years ago I received a pitch from an entrepreneur wanting me to invest $500,000 into his startup. The potential upside sounded incredible based on his projections. But you know what? I didn't even seriously consider it for a second. Because his pitch materials contained zero acknowledgment of how he'd make things right if the company flamed out disastrously. No skin in the game, no remorse management plan, no assurances I wouldn't end up holding the regretful bag while he skipped town with my capital.

To wealthy buyers, that kind of pitch devoid of meaningful guardrails enabling their certainty around a satisfactory outcome - even if things go awry - reads as a bright red amateur con flag. They simply won't take meetings or progress discussions without that foundational satisfaction covered from the start.

Now take the opposite approach where I've brought affluent clients into my high-end tailoring house to design fully customized wardrobes. Even though the prices are lavish, there's zero uncertainty because I control the entire experience end-to-end and set exacting expectations:

"I'm sourcing these exquisite Italian fabrics specifically for your suits. I'll be managing your fittings with my most experienced tailors to ensure your ideal customized fit and styling. Any adjustments or tweaks until you're 100% satisfied are included. If anything turns out not impeccable, I'll remake the pieces from scratch or whatever it takes until you're blown away. This isn't some factory production, this is an artisan covenant between us."

See how that conveys complete certainty and satisfaction guaranteed despite the premium pricing? There's no chance of an unsavory outcome invalidating their investment because I've already pre-sold accountability and personal responsibility for ensuring their fulfillment.

For wealthy buyers, that assuredness is utterly paramount. Which is why premium luxury brands like Ritz Carlton train employees to say "My pleasure" instead of "You're welcome." It's a subtle yet potent way of reassuring guests they have the service's full control, avenues of certainty supplied for any foreseeable hiccup that could disappoint.

When soliciting the affluent, this ethos of disappointment avoidance should permeate every aspect of your messaging, offer design, and sales approach. Make it a visceral priority to pre-emptively identify and install exhaustive guarantees, satisfaction assurances, and remorse management systems that grant your prospects much-needed certainty from square one.

It could be a money-back guarantee or investment buyback like the crypto example. Maybe it's overcompensation policies for any mistakes. Perhaps you pioneer new technologies, processes, or staffing roles exclusively devoted to ensuring predictable premium experiences. The form matters less than institutionalizing this assuredness as your brand's backbone from Day 1.

For premium providers and luxury sellers, disappointment cannot be an option - ever. Your offers must be

Anti-Bum Shield

crafted, sold, and delivered as unassailable bastions of certainty regardless of any external circumstances. Instill that philosophy as the foundational core of your brand's very existence.

See, wealthy buyers aren't simply purchasing your basic products or services - they're investing in an elevated, stress-free experience where literally every conceivable expectation is met or exceeded. Any potential for disappointment or dissatisfaction must be systematically eliminated before they'll even entertain opening their wallets.

That's the uncompromising mental model you need to inhabit when courting the affluent. You're not just a service provider or seller - you're an elite experience concierge whose personal credibility is 100% attached to delivering perfectly on exacting promises. Fail that covenant in any capacity, and you've not only lost the business, but damaged your reputation as a reliable luxury purveyor permanently.

Sounds like a lot of pressure, right? It absolutely is, and that's precisely why the wealthy are willing to pay exponential premiums to the few brands and individuals who can supply that certainty. They're investing in a hassle-free outcome, not whatever generic offering or commodity could potentially disappoint them like every other letdown in their opulent lives.

The bar for earning and keeping their partnership is stratospherically high - but the rewards for clearing it are equally limitless. Consistently amaze them with your accountability and satisfaction principles in action, and affluent spenders will quite literally give you the keys to their kingdoms (and finances) as long as you preserve that covenant.

For example, let's say you provide in-home personal training and nutrition coaching for elite professionals and celebrities. Are you going to pitch them some generic twice-weekly session package like any other trainer? Of course not! You need to design and sell a full-service lifestyle optimization program guaranteeing comprehensive results:

"For the ultimate investment of $100,000 per year, you'll receive my White Glove Bio-Hacking treatment. I'll embed a private chef and dietician in your home full-time to uphold your customized nutrition protocols. My experienced staff will handle all your grocery procurement and meal prep work so you never have to think about it. You'll have 24/7 access to book any

Anti-Bum Shield

workout session type with my elite trainers based on your dynamically evolving needs...

And that's just the start - we'll also fully optimize your sleep environment, manage your daily supplement regimen, provide massage therapy and cryogenic recovery, apply the latest wearable bio-tracking tech, and more. If at any point your body recomposition results from our program aren't exceeding expectations, you can terminate our engagement and receive a full refund..."

See how that transforms your services into a comprehensive luxury experience underwritten by your personal assurance of stellar outcomes or else? You're alleviating every potential headache, uncertainty, and grievance before it can happen - and backing it with skin in the game.

For the wealthy, that's a bargain at virtually any price point. Because you're delivering the vitally precious currency of uncompromised experiences free of disappointment, a scarcity most luxury goods still can't consistently supply. When your brand represents that level of selectively elevated hospitality and service for their desires, you become irresistible to those who place your sacred assurances over common commodities.

The key is designing your entire operation as a seamless conduit for their deterministic gratification from square one, not an assortment of disparate services that could let disappointment sneak into the experience anywhere. You're selling predictable perfection wrapped in your personal staffing, expertise, and systematic processes to ensure it - not hoping your basic offerings simply achieve adequate outcomes.

Craft that disappointment-proof experience ecosystem for your ideal clientele's aspirations, and you'll be able to better perceive monetary exchange for your servant value delivery isn't a protracted transaction - it's their privileged grantsmanship into the certainty of satisfaction they crave above all else.

Does this approach require more diligent design and operational intensity from you as the premium provider? Absolutely - but that's the price of admission into the wealthy's world, where average results and services will render you an extinction-bound commodity in their unblinking assessments.

Anti-Bum Shield

The sooner you accept that gratifying the rich demands fanatical adherence to preemptive satisfaction principles above all else, the sooner you can start commanding their dollars without objection. Because once your brand becomes synonymous with the enjoying luxuries of predictable, hassle-free experiences - money objections dissipate almost entirely.

Why? Because you've eliminated their biggest fear factor: disappointment and uncertainty around receiving anything less than impeccable results. You're no longer soliciting payment for basic products or services that could letdown. You're facilitating their privileged access into an elevated plane where perfect satisfaction is the only acceptable outcome, underwritten by your obsessive orchestration.

At that point, pricing discussions transform from combative barter sessions into simple formalities - because value & cost calculations are irrelevant when the certainty you're providing is priceless to those who appreciate it. You've established yourself as the charismatic orchestrator of sublime encounters free of compromise, not just another commodity service provider incapable of ensuring that predictability.

For premium consumers, that's the dream engagement: no guesswork, no wonder if things will measure up, no risk of valuable hours or dollars having been wasted on overhyped mediocrity. Just a turnkey extraordinary experience facilitated by a best-in-class host they can blindly entrust with delivering on their exacting standards.

Key Ideas of Chapter Three

1. Affluent buyers want to avoid disappointment and wasted time more than anything else.

2. Provide ironclad assurances and guarantees of satisfaction to give them the certainty they crave.

3. Design your entire offering to proactively eliminate any possibility of a subpar experience.

4. Hold yourself accountable for delivering flawless results, not just providing a service.

5. Command premium prices by ensuring predictably exceptional outcomes, not selling commodities.

Questions for self-development

- Am I really guaranteeing wealthy clients a disappointment-proof experience with my offerings?

- Where are the potential gaps that could allow for subpar service delivery or unmet expectations?

- How can I better institutionalize uncompromising standards of satisfaction into my processes?

- Am I still selling my offerings as standalone services vs. fully-managed premium experiences?

- Do I have enough skin in the game to assure affluent buyers I'm fully accountable for results?

- How can I make pricing a trivial afterthought by providing priceless certainty of outcome?

- What would need to change to make my brand synonymous with predictable perfection?

Chapter 4: Monetary relationships and benefits

At the heart of every profitable business lies an uncomfortable truth: Making money has little to do with providing what customers need, and everything to do with giving them what they desperately want right now.

Take the example of a personal trainer or fitness coach. Their biggest fear is that the training will become a dreary chore for the client, something they resent doing. So the smart move is to make the experience as engaging and addictive as possible - even if that means going against your "expert" instincts about what's optimal.

Instead of grinding through textbook perfect workouts, you make it spontaneous and gamelike. You tease and push and pull, always leaving them wanting more, not less. When they're riding the high of endorphins and adrenaline, you call it quits for the day while they're still hungry. Leave 'em begging to come back for another hit.

Is that the "right" way to get them in shape by the book? Probably not. But it IS the right way to keep them happily paying and showing up. Because at the end of the day, the market doesn't give a damn about your expertise or their genuine needs. It responds to cravings and desires, period.

This can be a tough pill to swallow for well-meaning professionals used to playing the wise guru. We like to think we know better, that we're guiding people to make optimal choices for their own good. But that's just a comforting myth we tell ourselves. If the customer's current itch is at odds with our vision of what they "should" want, nine times out of ten, the itch wins.

Just look at how much cash people gleefully set on fire "investing" in speculative crypto shitcoins and NFTs, even as financial advisors tear their hair out warning it will end in tears. Or the hordes of folks forking over their savings to whatever fad diet or detox is dominating the bestseller lists and social feeds this month.

Is any of that stuff in their TRUE best interest, by any rational analysis? Doubtful. But it speaks to the white-hot DESIRES raging in their minds and hearts at this moment. And those desires will always, always trump sober lectures about what's sensible or healthy or wise.

As entrepreneurs, we can either rage against that primal tide like petulant children, or learn to surf it like savvy adults. The ones who stubbornly insist on force-feeding people what they "ought" to want based on some moral high ground inevitably go broke. The ones who get really fucking good at serving up what the masses are already craving inevitably get paid.

Sometimes that means letting go of your precious ideals about delivering capital-V "Value" and just giving the people what they want, full stop. Other times it means finding clever ways to trojan horse your deeper wisdom into solutions to their surface level demands.

Like packaging your hard-won expertise on holistic nutrition and lifestyle design as a "6 Pack Abs in 60 Days" challenge, because that's the outcome a huge chunk of your market is actively drooling over. Is it the most profound or complete way to upgrade their health and wellbeing? No. But it IS the hook that will motivate them to actually open their wallets and implement your protocols.

And once you've banked that goodwill and trust by making good on your flashy promise, you've earned the right to start gradually expanding their perspective and steering them to embrace your bigger picture

Anti-Bum Shield

philosophies on their own time. The abs were the ethical bribe to get your foot in the psychological door. What you do beyond that is the real work.

Or take the case of a Fortune 500 executive making bank but drowning in stress, anxiety and overwhelm. You COULD come at him with your elaborate theories on the perils of acute cortisol and pitch some lofty 3-month sabbatical to realign his chakras and rewrite his limiting beliefs.

But he'd probably look at you like you just stepped out a UFO, because none of that highfalutin stuff maps to his current BURNING DESIRE - which is to simply stop dreading the 5,000 unread emails waiting for him every Monday morning. He just wants to be able to unplug over the weekend without his blood pressure spiking, not embark on some new age vision quest.

So you table your grandest ideas and instead offer him the "Inbox Zero in 90 Days" VIP intensive to eradicate his most acute pain point and get him the quickest, most concrete win. THEN, once you've delivered on that modest promise and earned his trust, you can start slipping in your more holistic strategies and inviting him to level up. It's a dance, a seduction, not a lecture or debate.

Because here's the uncomfortable reality: Unless you're already a mega celebrity in your space, the vast majority of your potential clients DO NOT CARE about your mighty expertise or thought leadership out of the gate. They're not in the market for a guru, they're in the market for a result, an outcome, a solution to what's making them BLEED right this minute.

And the businesses that win - ethically, might I add - are the ones who get fanatically attuned to sniffing out those real-time bleeding neck wounds and offering themselves up as the perfect gauze. They don't waste cycles trying to convince the market to want something more high-minded or refined. They go where the demand already IS, in all its raw urgency, and focus monomaniacally on becoming the go-to source for fast, effective relief.

Yes, along the way, they absolutely weave in their broader insights and philosophies to leave the customer better off than they found them. Like the trainer who DOES slip in serious nutrition and recovery protocols on the back end of the beach bod program. Or the executive coach who DOES introduce meditation and journaling into the inbox taming process.

Anti-Bum Shield

But they're not LEADING with that stuff or making it the star of the show. They're not expecting the market to spontaneously combust with desire for it just because it's quote-unquote "good for them." They're simply using it as seasoning for the main course the customer is already salivating for.

And because they're so skilled at delivering that main course - the six pack, the empty inbox, whatever - at a world-class level, the customer WILLINGLY embraces the deeper stuff. It becomes a welcome addon, not an unwanted sermon. And that willing embrace is what opens the door to true transformation and trust over time. You gotta earn the right to preach, not the other way around.

Does this mean you have to dumb down your message or become some carnival barker slinging superficial crap you don't believe in? Hell no. You can be a connoisseur and still cook for the common man. It just takes a shift from imposing your worldview to TRANSLATING it to mesh with where folks are at right this moment.

It means starting every new product or service design by asking: What are the most URGENT pains and unmet desires rampaging through my market TODAY? Not someday. TODAY. What outcomes and experiences are they already reaching for their wallets to buy, even if it's not the "best" thing for them long term? That's your cue, your opening, your back door to making a real mark.

Then it's on you to get world-class at providing those outcomes in a way that also slips in your higher wisdom and gently guides them to a better path - without making them eat their veggies like a mean mommy. Not by tricking them, but by TIMING your teachings to sync with their current psychological readiness.

Some might say this is playing to the lowest common denominator or enabling bad behavior. And sure, in clumsy or careless hands, it can be. But intent matters. If your genuine goal is to meet people where they are so you can usher them someplace higher over time, then giving them what they crave is an act of compassion, not cynicism. It's how you go from resented scold to welcomed sherpa.

Of course, this assumes two things:

Anti-Bum Shield

One, that you actually give enough of a shit about your audience to take the time to UNDERSTAND their real felt needs and complex humanity before passing judgment and imposing prescriptions.

And two, that you actually possess the rare SKILL required to deliver the specific results they're craving at a "holy shit, this is amazing!" level, not just pay lip service while ramming your own agenda down their throat.

That's where 99% of wannabe experts and gurus fall flat on their face, because they're too busy sniffing their own moral farts to bother being useful in the ways that MATTER to those they claim to serve. Then they wonder why their noble efforts are met with crickets and exasperated eye rolls.

But the REAL pros, the ones who thrive for years and decades? They're the ones who put their egos and ideologies aside and find a way to make their medicine go down like honey, by wrapping it in whatever spoonful of sugar the customer already has a sweet tooth for.

They don't strong-arm, they SURVEY. They don't scold, they SEDUCE. They don't pander, they PAVE a smart path from a to z by walking a mile in their prospect's itchy, unsatisfied shoes.

And because of that intense, almost psychic level of market intimacy and problem-solving prowess, they are WELCOMED into hearts and minds as the missing key, not resented as sanctimonious scolds on the sidelines.

So if you REALLY want to eradicate scarcity and struggle and create the business and life you're meant for? Get fucking OBSESSED with understanding the true, unspoken hungers clawing at your people in the wee hours of the night. The hungers they can't even fully articulate yet, but you can SENSE through the tenor of their demands and frustrations.

Then stop at nothing to feed those hungers like no one else alive, WHILE baking in your higher insights in a way that expands their beliefs and behaviors almost imperceptibly over time.

THAT is how you become irreplaceable, irresistible, damn near worship-worthy in your sphere of genius.

Anti-Bum Shield

Not by lecturing from on high, but by entering the cave of their current cravings and proving you have the most effective, ecstatic exits to the light - as THEY define it first, then you redefine it as you go.

Anything less is just mental masturbation masquerading as a business or a "calling." And the graveyard of entrepreneurs is littered with the bones of stubborn purists who thought they could bend the market to their infallible will.

No, no, no, my clever friend. The great ones - in business, in art, in leadership, in LIFE - are the ones with the wisdom and humility to let the market bend THEM to its will FIRST. And then, slowly but surely, flip the script on what's possible through the sheer, undeniable thunder of their RESULTS.

So tell me - which will you be? The irrelevant blowhard shaking your fist at the fickle mob?

Or the benevolent beast who earns the right to LEAD them to higher ground by first serving up their heart's every dark and dirty desire... better, faster and more exquisitely than the other carnival barkers EVER dreamed? Choose wisely.

Key Ideas of Chapter Four

1. Focus on addressing the most urgent, visceral cravings of your market, not just textbook needs.

2. Discover the hidden desires and fears driving your prospect's behavior and buying choices.

3. Become world-class at delivering the results they want NOW, then integrate your deeper solutions.

4. Targeting either the luxury market or the mass market can be more profitable than aiming for the middle market, which is fraught with challenges and inconsistencies.

5. Translate your expertise into forms that directly mesh with their current pains and goals.

6. Earn the right to lead customers to higher ground by first indulging their felt wants masterfully.

Questions for self-development

- Am I trying to impose my ideas of what customers "should" want or serving their raw desires?

Anti-Bum Shield

- Do I really understand the secret cravings and frustrations driving my market's behavior?

- How can I reframe my offerings to directly speak to their most urgent, visceral "itches"?

- Am I investing in becoming the best in the world at scratching those itches or lecturing from afar?

- Where am I stubbornly leading with my expertise vs. earning trust with quick, craved wins?

- How can I make my "medicine" feel indulgent by mixing it with what they already find delicious?

- Am I willing to put my ego aside and meet them where they are or arrogantly demand obedience?

- Do the products or services I use cater more to the luxury market, the mass market, or somewhere in between? How has their market positioning affected my satisfaction and my perception of their value?

Chapter 5: "Money place" and opportunities

Anti-Bum Shield

Money and success don't just magically appear out of thin air. They tend to pool in very specific places where ambitious people congregate - what I call "money places." Your job is to identify those lucrative hubs, get yourself in the middle of the action, and start soaking up the opportunities swirling around until you're drenched.

But it's not enough to just show up in these environments. You need to fully immerse yourself, make your presence known, and actively angle to create and capitalize on profitable connections and deals. The real players make it their mission to become an indispensable fixture in those circles. They're not just observing from the sidelines.

For example, I had an open invitation to speak at Alfa Group, a major Russian banking conglomerate. Sounds like a prime opportunity to get in front of some heavyweight decision-makers, right? Well, I turned it down without a second thought. Why? Because I wasn't personally invited by an internal champion who genuinely wanted me there.

See, even when infiltrating "money places," you need to be strategic about which rooms you walk into. If you're just a warm body to fill an agenda that no one's excited about, your presence and message will have zero impact. You're a court jester, not an influential voice.

On the flip side, when you've cultivated the relationships and reputation to be specifically requested by the power players, you wield serious sway in those environments. You're not just a forgettable speaker - you're a prized resource whose perspective is hungrily consumed by the audience.

Developing that VIP clout within "money places" takes a combination of networking savvy, unassailable credibility, and a keen understanding of the hidden desires driving the influencers you're engaging with. It's about figuring out their psychological pressure points and positioning yourself as an indispensable asset for resolving them.

I had a wealthy construction mogul in Moscow constantly angling to spend time with me. This guy was hinting at ultra-lucrative consulting engagements, practically begging to deposit heaps of cash just to be around me and soak up my knowledge. But in my inexperienced naivety, I was too dense to recognize the incredible education and connections that relationship

Anti-Bum Shield

could have unlocked. I foolishly brushed him off to stick to my routine.

Looking back, it makes me cringe at the wasted potential. Getting close to a titan like that would have given me a first-class pass to witness the inner workings of serious money and power, not to mention a ticket to any door I wanted to walk through in that scene. Even if I never directly monetized the intel, the experience and social proof would have catapulted my stature immensely.

Once you hit "insider" status within a "money place," the floodgates of opportunity swing wide open. You're no longer a vendor or hanger-on - you're a verified value-adder with a rolodex (contact list) of power players eager to do business. That reputational boost serves as a magnet for premium clients and partnerships average entrepreneurs can only fantasize about.

But ascending to that rarefied air isn't a passive process. You can't just timidly orbit the edges hoping mega-deals land in your lap by association. The name of the game is proactively identifying the right rooms, earning your way in through relentless value-adding and unimpeachable credibility-building, and then capitalizing ruthlessly once you've got a seat at the table.

Too many would-be entrepreneurs delude themselves thinking they can manifest big success by heads-down grinding solo. They dream of toiling away unseen and then bursting onto the scene with an overnight windfall that shocks the world. But that Lone Wolf lottery ticket almost never pays off.

In reality, the entrepreneurial icons are perpetually entrenched in the "money place" ecosystems crucial to their industries. They're forging alliances, spotting synergies, and architecting blockbuster ventures by combining their assets, connections and visions in potent configurations simply not possible in isolation.

Take the time I had an out-of-the-blue offer from a wealthy guy to pay me €50,000 to intensely pick my brain for 3 days straight, staying with me to study how I operate. On its face, that seems like a no-brainer cash grab for sharing knowledge I could do in my sleep. But something in my gut made me press pause.

Now, perhaps to my financial detriment, I told him to slow his roll, really dig into my free content first to see if he vibed with my style, and then decide if a deep dive made sense. Unsurprisingly, he evaporated and

Anti-Bum Shield

the €50K with him. But it illuminated an important distinction in "money place" mechanics.

See, high-caliber players in those ponds aren't looking to impulsively throw stacks at anyone with a half-baked value prop. They're aiming to invest in strategic partnerships with practitioners who intimately grasp their specific context and can tailor bespoke solutions to their most labyrinthine problems. They don't want drive-by consulting - they want to make focused allies.

So while part of me definitely regrets leaving that short-term cash on the table, I know deep down it was the proper chess move for the long game I'm playing. Flash in the pan gigs are a dime a dozen once you're a known quantity in the right circles. But carefully cultivated relationships rooted in trust and generous value creation are the real skeleton key.

Does this mean you need to be some sleazy glad-hander to thrive in "money place" environments? Not at all. In fact, power players can smell an obsequious (excessive flattery) snake from a mile away and will have you blackballed with the quickness. Influence peddlers who reek of self-serving smarminess get shot down before ever breaching the gates.

To really excel in those ecosystems, you need to arrive as a force in your own right. Someone with unassailable competence, rock-solid offerings, and the gravitas to garner respect from big dogs. Anything less and you'll get eaten alive before ever getting past the velvet rope.

So if you're serious about staking your claim in "money place" meccas, it's time to go all-in. No more tentatively sniffing around the fringes or meekly trying to get noticed. You need to barge into those rooms with the bulletproof confidence and congruence of a VIP who knows beyond a doubt they're supposed to be there.

Will it be nerve-wracking at first? Almost certainly. Nothing worthwhile comes easy, especially in cutthroat arenas where fortunes are won and lost. But with unflappable belief in your capacity to deliver value and the initiative to create your own luck, there's no ceiling on how high you can rise.

A great example of this is when I started advertising personal training sessions at the gym when I was just 16. I threw up a post on a local classifieds site with my

Anti-Bum Shield

rates, figuring I had nothing to lose. Well, a friend of mine who was a European kickboxing champ saw the ad and confronted me: "Are you crazy? What if I show up and beat you up to show you you're not qualified?"

My response? "Feel free to do it if you genuinely think I'm not worth the price I'm charging. In fact, I invite you to put up your own ads for 5-10X the rate if you believe that's what the market will bear. Doesn't matter to me either way. I'm confident I'm providing fair value for fair pay and am happy for clients to be the ultimate judge."

See, even as a teenager, I intuitively understood something most entrepreneurs never grasp - your pricing is an expression of your unapologetically honest assessment of the ROI you deliver for the customer, not some internally negotiated compromise based on insecurity or scarcity.

If you're perpetually second-guessing your worth relative to others in your space, you've already lost before setting foot in a "money place." The true rainmakers operate from a place of rock-solid belief in their problem-solving power, and allow the market to determine acceptable thresholds from there.

Showing up to wealth-ridden rooms with even a whiff of self-doubt about your right to be there is a one-way ticket to the kids' table. Save the imposter syndrome for your therapy sessions. Between those walls, you either arrive as a peer ready to play or find yourself on the outside looking in faster than you can do the math on how much your hesitancy just cost you.

So the next time you feel that flicker of anxiety about asserting your value in a "money place," remember - your worth isn't up for discussion. It's a self-evident fact to be demonstrated through unapologetic offers and invitations for qualified buyers to step up. You can't claim a seat at the big table while secretly feeling you don't deserve to be waited on.

Whether you're selling personal training sessions, brokering eight-figure deals, or anything in between, the game is the same. Identify the "money places" where your ideal prospects congregate, infiltrate with the bulletproof conviction of an apex predator who's generous with value but avoids no one, and then make your ambitious asks with the unwavering faith of someone who knows the universe itself wants them to have everything they desire.

Anti-Bum Shield

That combination of giving from abundance, playing win/win, and refusing to apologize for claiming your piece of the pie is the foolproof skeleton key for turning any "money place" into your personal cash machine. But it all starts with that internal upgrade from self-doubting pauper to self-assured prince.

Everything else - the relationships, the respect, the unthinkable rewards - naturally falls into place from there. You just have to find the spine to step into your self-appointed birthright. No one's going to hand it to you unearned. In "money places" and in life, either bet on yourself at the level you want reciprocated or don't be surprised when no one else will either. There is no middle ground.

Key Ideas of Chapter Five

1. Identify and immerse yourself in the key "money places" in your industry or niche.

2. Engaging with an audience that has personally chosen you can lead to more meaningful and impactful interactions than speaking to an assigned audience.

3. Focusing on clients who perceive higher value in your services and are willing to pay premium prices can enhance profitability and satisfaction.

4. Build VIP clout by combining networking, credibility and keen understanding of player psychologies.

5. Take initiative to find and capitalize on the best opportunities, don't wait passively.

6. Show up with unshakable confidence in your worth and right to be there among the top tier.

Questions for self-development

- Have I ever missed an opportunity because I underestimated my value or did not present myself confidently? What can I learn from that experience?

Anti-Bum Shield

- What are the key "money places" in my field and am I positioning myself at the heart of them?

- How can I cultivate the relationships and reputation to be sought out by the heavy hitters?

- Am I being strategic enough about which opportunities I pursue or haphazardly chasing sparkly objects?

- Where am I still thinking like a timid outsider trying to slip in vs. a VIP who belongs in the room?

Chapter 6: Sensing people. Tactfulness

Anti-Bum Shield

Being a master technician in your field is just the price of entry if you want to build a thriving business or career. The real fortunes are reserved for those who can artfully navigate human psychology and engineer win-win deals by sensing people's true needs and leveraging that knowledge with tact and nuance.

Consider my friend, a brilliant specialist who consistently delivers top-notch work. You'd think he's got it made - a skill set that's second to none and the track record to prove it. But he's perpetually stuck under a glass ceiling, struggling to reach his full potential professionally. Why? Because his people skills are completely tone-deaf.

Sure, he can execute on the technical side better than anyone. But when it comes to interpersonal finesse - reading between the lines, adjusting his approach to different personality types, knowing how to structure sensitive conversations for maximum impact - he's like a bull in a china shop. He's missing the crucial X-factor that turns competence into true influence.

For example, when it comes to discussing pricing and payment, Armen has the subtlety of a hand grenade. He robotically sticks to a rigid one size-fits-all script regardless of who he's talking to or their unique context. There's no attempt to thoughtfully match the value prop to their individual desires and pressure points. He just clumsily blurts out his generic pitch and hopes something sticks.

In doing so, he's leaving fortunes on the table. See, prospects are constantly sizing you up, revealing key intel about how they operate. It's on you to intercept those tells and cater accordingly. If you're speaking to a client who casually throws around huge numbers, trying to nickle and dime them with a anemic (weak) offer is a fantastic way to torpedo the relationship. They'll write you off as a unsophisticated amateur not worth their time.

Instead, when engaging with big fish, you need to rise to the occasion. Recognize their desire for a premium white-glove experience and position yourself as the comprehensive solution to their most complex challenges. Don't just pitch a simple service, invite them on a transformational journey that speaks to their loftiest ambitions.

On the flip side, not every prospect needs or wants the full court press. If you're interfacing with a bootstrapper whose primary concern is maximizing limited resources, force-feeding them a caviar experience when they just want dependable value will freeze them in their tracks. You need to dial back the intensity and demonstrate how partnering with you is the high ROI move based on their specific definition of success.

The trick is having the emotional intelligence to coldly read people and seamlessly adapt your approach to resonate with their hard-wiring. Think of it like a dance - you're vibing off your partner's moves, not just robotically cycling through a pre-set routine oblivious to their reactions. If you're not fluidly adjusting to the dynamic, the whole exchange feels clunky and stilted. No one's eager for a repeat performance.

Or think of it like a wrestling match. You can know all the sickest moves, have the slickest techniques drilled into muscle memory. But if you're on autopilot just waiting for chances to bust out your pet maneuvers, you're going to get wrecked. Success hinges on your ability to anticipate the opponent's shifts, capitalize on their momentary vulnerabilities, and chain attacks that compound on each other. You need to be three steps ahead, playing mental chess while they're still processing the last parry.

That level of instinctive responsiveness is what separates the journeymen from the rainmakers. When you can sniff out someone's driving desires, secret fears, and unspoken reservations in real time and craft perfectly pitched solutions on the fly, you become irresistible. People melt in the face of feeling intimately understood. Checkbooks fly open with scarcely a nudge.

But if you're ham-fistedly barreling through tone-deaf pitches without any attempt to relate... forget about it. Nothing telegraphs "I don't really get you and am just here to extract value" quite like an oblivious steamrolling. Even if the underlying substance is solid, the vibe will be irreparably contaminated.

Now, this isn't about becoming some sort of manipulation wizard. It's not about mind games or underhanded persuasion hacks. In fact, it's the opposite - when you're truly attuned to someone and speaking to their authentic needs, you can be more direct and honest than ever. The permission to be upfront expands in direct proportion to the strength of the bond.

It's actually clumsy, artless selling that relies on cheap psychological parlor tricks. Genuinely understanding people's core drivers and reflecting them back with compassion is the furthest thing from slimy. It's the essence of good business - create an offer that scratches their itch better than they even knew they needed, deliver it in terms custom fit to their quirks, and do it all in a way that demonstrates you have their best interests in mind.

So if you want to thrive in high stakes people-driven environments, forget the corny closing techniques and manipulative zigzags. Throw away the generic scripts you're hiding behind. Commit to learning the lost art of astute people-reading and human-to-human calibration. Train your innate emotional intelligence the way a pro athlete relentlessly hones their sport-specific skills.

Start paying obsessive attention to all the subtle cues and micro-expressions that signal what's really going on under the hood for folks. Make it a game to guess their backstories, predict their objections, and divine the perfect thing to say to make them light up. Not so you can dupe them, but because your fascination with understanding and uplifting people runs so deep, you can't help but flex that muscle.

With enough practice, you'll develop an almost eerie ability to click with perfect strangers and make them feel like you're the only one who truly gets them. You'll know how to effortlessly modulate between disarming charm and unflappable authority. You'll sense with uncanny intuition who wants the Cadillac plan and who needs a sensible starter package. And you'll do it all with a twinkle in your eye that says "this is fun for me."

That's when you'll realize you've officially vaulted from the world of stale, Paint-by-Numbers business into the rarefied air of bespoke value creation. That glorious zone where your every interaction is an adventure in rapid-fire rapport-building. Where your income level has more to do with the depth of your people-whispering powers than the amount of information you wield.

Tactics and techniques will always have a place in your toolkit. But your real edge will be a bone-deep understanding of human drives and the improvisational wit to spin up miraculously attuned solutions at a moment's notice. You'll know you've arrived when your "sales pitch" is indistinguishable from an intimate heart-to-heart with an old friend. And your calendar is full of people thrilled to pay a king's ransom for the privilege.

Anti-Bum Shield

All because you took the time to decode the operating systems of everyone you meet and tailor your approach accordingly. In business and in life, that's as close to a superpower as mere mortals can hope to wield. So get out there and start wizening up to the wondrous, infuriating, endlessly fascinating code of Man. Your bank account and your legacy will thank you in ways you can't yet imagine.

Key Ideas of Chapter Six

1. Interpersonal finesse and tactical communication are as crucial as raw technical competence.

2. Astutely read between the lines to discern people's unspoken needs, fears and motivations.

3. Flexibly customize your approach and offer to align with each prospect's specific success criteria.

4. Hone your emotional intelligence to build rapid rapport and affinity with a wide range of people.

5. Aim to intimately understand and uplift others, not to manipulate or deceive for personal gain.

Questions for self-development

- Am I overly reliant on generic scripts vs. attuning to each person's unique psychological blueprint?

- How can I sharpen my ability to read subtle nonverbal cues and detect what's unsaid?

- Where am I leaving money on the table by not customizing my approach for different audiences?

Anti-Bum Shield

- Do I make others feel deeply understood and valued or like I'm robotically going through the motions?

- How can I practice building faster, deeper rapport and connection with a wider range of people?

- Am I hiding behind tactics and techniques or tapping into authentic human-to-human resonance?

- If I had an almost psychic ability to sense people's true needs, how would my communication change?

Chapter 7: Benefit Does Not Equal Money

Anti-Bum Shield

Buckle up, because we're about to shatter a pervasive myth that keeps far too many entrepreneurs and business owners trapped in a cycle of frustration and underearning. It's a belief that's been hammered into our heads since childhood, but it's time to face the cold, hard truth: In the real world, the amount of benefit you provide has absolutely zero correlation with the amount of money you can charge.

I know, I know - it's a tough pill to swallow. We all want to believe that we live in a just and rational economic system where the most valuable products and services are automatically rewarded with the highest prices. But if that were true, teachers and surgeons would be driving Ferraris while reality TV stars and influencers scraped by on minimum wage.

The fact is, we don't live in that imaginary world, no matter how much we might wish we did. And the sooner you accept that reality and start playing by the actual rules of the game, the sooner you can start earning what you're truly worth.

Let me give you a concrete example. A skilled surgeon might spend hours meticulously operating on a patient, literally saving their life in the process. For this incredible feat of expertise and high-stakes benefit, they might earn a modest salary of $150,000 per year.

Meanwhile, a top football player like Lionel Messi can earn upwards of $40 million per year - not for saving lives, but for kicking a ball around a field and starring in some commercials. Is Messi's contribution to society 266 times more valuable than the surgeon's? Of course not. But that's the economic reality we live in.

The same principle applies across every industry and niche. You could be the most skilled, experienced, and beneficial service provider in your field, but if you don't understand how to package, position, and price your offerings in a way that aligns with your target market's value hierarchy, you'll always be stuck earning a fraction of what you deserve.

I've seen it happen time and time again. A brilliant software developer pours their heart and soul into creating an app that genuinely makes people's lives easier, but they price it at $0.99 in the App Store because they don't want to be "greedy." Meanwhile, a flashy startup with a fraction of the functionality charges $100/month for their inferior product and rakes in millions.

It's not fair, but it's the truth. And the sooner you accept it and start working with it instead of against it, the sooner you can break free from the shackles of underearning and start commanding the prices you deserve.

So how do you do that? It all comes down to understanding and aligning with your target market's unique value hierarchy. Every individual has their own internal system for determining what something is worth to them, based on a complex web of beliefs, experiences, and emotions.

Your job as a business owner or entrepreneur is to deeply understand that value hierarchy and position your offerings in a way that speaks directly to it. It's not about convincing them to adopt your value system - it's about shaping your messaging and positioning to align with theirs.

For example, let's say you're trying to sell a high-end coaching program to busy executives. You could focus your messaging on the objective benefits of your program - the proven strategies, the tangible results, the ROI. And for some prospects, that might be enough to get them to pull the trigger.

But for others, the real value lies in the status and prestige of working with an exclusive, in-demand coach. They want to feel like they're part of an elite inner circle, rubbing elbows with other top performers and industry leaders. They're not just buying coaching - they're buying a identity and a feeling of superiority.

If you understand that value hierarchy and shape your messaging and positioning accordingly, you can charge premium prices that align with the perceived value you're creating. It's not about being manipulative or deceptive - it's about understanding what really matters to your ideal clients and delivering on that in spades.

Of course, this isn't always easy. It requires a deep level of empathy, a willingness to really listen and observe, and a commitment to continually refining your approach based on feedback and results. But the payoff is immense - not just in terms of your bottom line, but in terms of your impact and fulfillment as well.

When you're able to charge prices that truly reflect the value you're creating, you're able to invest more into your business, your team, and your own growth and development. You're able to take on fewer clients and go deeper with each one, creating transformational experiences that leave a lasting impact. You're able to build a sustainable, thriving business that supports your lifestyle and your vision for the future.

But none of that is possible if you're still clinging to the myth that benefit equals money. It's a limiting belief that will keep you stuck in a cycle of overwork and underearning, no matter how much value you're creating in the world.

So it's time to take a hard look at your own mindset and beliefs around pricing and value. Are you still subconsciously anchored to the idea that you can only charge what your offering is "objectively" worth? Are you afraid to raise your prices because you don't want to be seen as greedy or exclusionary?

If so, it's time to do the inner work necessary to break free from those limiting beliefs and step into your full power as a business owner and value creator. It won't be easy - those beliefs are often deeply ingrained and can be tough to shake loose. But the rewards are more than worth it.

One powerful exercise is to take a close look at some of the most successful products, services, and individuals in your industry - the ones who seem to effortlessly command premium prices and attract high-value clients. What are they doing differently from you? How are they positioning themselves and their offerings? What kind of language and messaging are they using?

Chances are, they've mastered the art of aligning with their target market's value hierarchy and creating perceived value that goes far beyond the objective benefits of what they're selling. They've learned how to tap into the deeper desires, aspirations, and emotional needs of their ideal clients, and they've built their entire brand and business around serving those needs at the highest level.

And here's the thing - there's no reason you can't do the same. It doesn't matter what industry you're in, what kind of products or services you offer, or how much experience you have. If you're willing to do the work to deeply understand your market and craft a compelling value proposition that speaks directly to their needs and desires, you can absolutely charge premium prices and build a thriving, impactful business.

But it all starts with letting go of the myth that benefit equals money. It's a comforting belief, but it's simply not true in the real world. And the sooner you accept that and start playing by the actual rules of the game, the sooner you can start living life on your own terms and making the impact you were born to make.

So how do you actually go about doing that? How do you figure out what your ideal clients really value, and how do you position your offerings in a way that speaks directly to those values?

It all starts with deep, empathetic listening. You need to be genuinely curious about your target market - what keeps them up at night, what they're struggling with, what they're hoping to achieve. You need to ask probing questions and really seek to understand their perspective, even if it's different from your own.

One powerful way to do this is through customer interviews. Reach out to a handful of your ideal clients (or potential clients) and ask if you can buy them a coffee and pick their brain for 30 minutes. Come prepared with a list of open-ended questions that get to the heart of what they value and what they're looking for in a product or service like yours.

For example, you might ask things like:

- "What's the biggest challenge you're facing in your business/life right now?"

- "What would your ideal solution to that challenge look like?"

- "What have you tried in the past to address this issue, and why didn't it work?"

- "What would success look like for you in this area, and what would that mean for your business/life?"

As you listen to their responses, pay attention not just to the words they're saying, but to the emotions and underlying desires behind those words. What are they really longing for? What are they afraid of? What do they value most?

You might start to notice patterns and themes emerging - certain phrases or ideas that come up again and again. These are clues to the value hierarchy that drives their decision-making, and they're incredibly valuable for shaping your messaging and positioning.

Anti-Bum Shield

For example, let's say you're a business coach who helps entrepreneurs scale their companies. You might notice that a lot of your ideal clients talk about feeling overwhelmed and stuck, like they're working harder than ever but not seeing the results they want. They might mention feeling like they're missing out on time with their families, or that they're not sure how to take their business to the next level.

Based on these insights, you might position your coaching program as the key to helping them break through their growth barriers, reclaim their time and freedom, and build a business that supports the lifestyle they want. You might use language like "scale with ease," "work smarter, not harder," and "achieve your boldest vision."

Notice how this messaging speaks directly to the values and desires that your ideal clients expressed - it's not just about the objective benefits of your program, but about the emotional and aspirational benefits as well.

Of course, customer interviews are just one way to gain these kinds of insights. You can also pay attention to the language and messaging used by your most successful competitors, or by thought leaders and influencers in your industry. You can survey your existing customers and ask for feedback on what they value most about your offerings. You can even use tools like social media listening to see what your target market is talking about online.

The key is to always be looking for clues and insights that help you better understand what your ideal clients really want and need, beyond just the surface-level benefits of your product or service. The more deeply you understand their value hierarchy, the more effectively you can position your offerings as the perfect solution to their most pressing problems and desires.

But here's the thing - this isn't a one-time exercise. Your target market's needs and values are constantly evolving, and what worked yesterday might not work tomorrow. You need to be continually listening, observing, and adapting based on what you learn.

This is where a lot of entrepreneurs and business owners get stuck. They come up with a messaging and positioning strategy that works for a while, and then they get complacent. They stop listening to their market, stop innovating and iterating, and before they know it, they're stuck in a rut of stagnant growth and dwindling profits.

Anti-Bum Shield

The most successful businesses are the ones that are always staying ahead of the curve, always looking for ways to better serve their market and deliver even more value. They're not afraid to pivot when necessary, to try new things and take calculated risks in pursuit of their vision.

And the good news is, when you're deeply attuned to your market's value hierarchy and consistently delivering on their most pressing needs and desires, those pivots and iterations become a lot less risky. You're not just guessing or throwing spaghetti at the wall - you're making informed, strategic decisions based on real data and insights.

So if you're feeling stuck or stagnant in your business right now, if you're struggling to attract high-value clients or command premium prices, take a step back and ask yourself - how well do I really understand my target market's value hierarchy? How effectively am I positioning my offerings to speak directly to their deepest needs and desires?

If the answer is "not very well" or "I'm not sure," don't beat yourself up - this is a common challenge for entrepreneurs at every stage of growth. The key is to commit to doing the work necessary to gain those insights and put them into action.

Start by reaching out to a few ideal clients and scheduling those customer interviews. Pay attention to the language and messaging being used by successful players in your industry. Survey your existing customers and ask for honest feedback on what they value most about your offerings.

And most importantly, don't be afraid to experiment and iterate based on what you learn. The path to premium prices and high-value clients is rarely a straight line - it's a winding road full of twists, turns, and unexpected detours. But if you stay committed to deeply understanding and serving your market at the highest level, you'll eventually arrive at your destination - a thriving, impactful business that supports your wildest dreams and ambitions.

So let go of the myth that benefit equals money, and start embracing the reality of your market's value hierarchy. It's not always easy, but it's the key to unlocking your full potential as an entrepreneur and making the impact you were born to make. You've got this - now go out there and make it happen.

Anti-Bum Shield

Key Ideas of Chapter Seven

1. Benefit provided does not equal money earned - pricing depends on perceived value.

2. Uncover your target market's unique value hierarchy and align your positioning with it.

3. Use empathetic listening and research to understand your ideal client's true wants and needs.

4. Craft messaging and offers that speak to emotional and aspirational desires, not just objective benefits.

5. Continually gather market insights, experiment, and adapt to stay ahead of evolving needs.

Questions for self-development

- Am I pricing based on the objective value I provide or my market's subjective perceptions?

- How well do I really understand what my ideal clients most want to feel and achieve?

- Does my messaging tap into the deeper emotional drivers behind purchase decisions?

- Am I positioning my offerings as premium solutions to my market's most pressing desires?

- When was the last time I interviewed customers to uncover changes in their value hierarchy?

- How can I gather better insights into what my market truly cares about and values?

- Where have I become complacent in my positioning vs. continually adapting to market needs?

Chapter 8: Business is a bluff

Anti-Bum Shield

Let's get brutally honest for a minute: the vast majority of businesses aren't really trading on some objective measure of value or benefit. They're peddling perceptions, narratives, and flat-out bluffs. The sooner you internalize that the game is won by the most convincing storytellers, not necessarily the most valid value props, the faster you can vault to the top.

Now, I know some of you self-appointed white knights are clutching your pearls and readying your lectures on integrity in business. You want to believe commerce is this rational, meritocratic exchange where the best products and services rise to the top on substance alone. Well I've got news for you - we're not in that world and never have been. We're in a world of smoke, mirrors, and the juiciest fictions.

Let me give you a raw example. Say you run a high-end retreat center peddling spiritual awakenings and personal breakthroughs. You're not really hawking cushions, incense and cafeteria grub. You're selling an intoxicating vision of what someone's life could become if they fork over five figures to play make-believe for a weekend. The actual logistics and material goods you provide? Window dressing to set the stage for the fantasy they're buying into.

Suppose a filthy rich corporate raider rolls up ready to blow some of his plunder on a vision quest. What's the "fair" price for his experience? If you said anything relating to your hard costs divided by an acceptable margin, you're not even playing the same sport, let alone in the right ballpark. The correct answer? Whatever he'll ecstatically pay based on the bluff you manage to sell.

So you get him suitably gassed up on live foods and half-baked mysticism. Wait for the perfect moment when his eyes are dilating and his chakras are tingling, and then You drop the REAL pitch: "Looks like you really got what you came for, boss! I'd love to take more of your money for this, but I've got other seekers to attend to. Maybe next time if you book wayyyy in advance and my calendar magically aligns, we can do this again."

BOOM! You've turned a one time transaction into an access-controlled asset he'll crawl over broken glass to attain again. And you did it by manufacturing scarcity and dangling the promise of more life-changing breakthroughs contingent on his buying power. Abracadabra, you just memed your little desert excursion into a velvet-roped, VIPs-only award in his mind. All

Anti-Bum Shield

without materially changing a thing about your actual offering.

THAT'S the power of bluffing in business. You can have the most humdrum, commodity products and services on the planet. But if you can spin an enchanting enough yarn about their worth and exclusivity, price becomes a mere triviality. People will find a way to give you wheelbarrows full of money just to bask in the warm glow of the shared hallucination you so deftly conjured.

Look at cryptocurrency for instance. Buncha nerds huddled around a blockchain making up magic monopoly money, right? HA! More like the greatest bluff ever sold. Early adopters weren't peddling digital tokens, they were peddling the STORY of an inevitably decentralized future where code cut out all the institutional middlemen. They repeated the mantras "currency of the future", "financial revolution", "web 3.0" enough times and the sheer audacity of the narrative took on a life of its own.

Fast forward a few years and suddenly even your Aunt Mildred is asking if she should have some of her pension in Bitcoin because she heard it was going to the moon on the Yahoo Finance ticker. No one actually

NEEDS crypto to conduct their daily affairs. But the collective fever dream was infectious enough to have people fighting for the right to exchange their labor for ones and zeroes some techie willed into existence on a distributed ledger.

That's the metagame of entrepreneurship no one tells you about when you're making your cute little lean canvas. Actual utility is maybe 20% of the battle at best. The rest is tribal affiliation, memetic virality, and shaping beliefs in the heads of your prospects. In a world of infinite options and limited attention, the most spellbinding shamans will always beat the most diligent bricklayers 9 times out of 10.

Even supposedly rational, sophisticated consumers fall prey to this all the time. You think that middle manager is signing off on a million dollar consulting contract because he's judiciously weighed all the options and done a sober cost/benefit? Please. He's thinking about the anecdote he can drop at the next executive retreat about bringing in the fanciest suits with the most prestigious logos. The LARP is what he's buying, not the actual PowerPoint slides.

Or take something as mundane as car buying. Sure, there's some element of objective comparison between makes and models - longevity, reliability, functionality, etc. But at the end of the day, the guy rolling off the lot in a new Benz isn't coldly calculating resale value and safety ratings. He's projecting a certain status and image to the world, and marinating in the unspoken cultural cache that comes with a hood ornament most can't afford.

Even the entertainment we choose operates on this level. When a company shells out seven figures for Sergey Svetlakov to come yuk it up at their year end function, they're not hiring the funniest or most original comic. They're renting the social proof and perceived cachet he's been anointed by mass media and popular opinion. They want their people to think "wow, they brought THE GUY. We must be big time players."

Meanwhile, true fans of the craft might find his whole schtick tired, derivative, practically automated at this point. But their opinion matters little in the grand scheme. The herd has chosen their golden clown, and his billed rate has little to do with actual merit. It's pure bluff buttressed by an aura of importance largely divorced from his moment to moment output.

Again, none of this is to say that there's no place for genuine craft, expertise, or substance in commerce. Of course those things matter on some profound level. All else being equal, the better offering should win out. But all else is so seldom equal that it's borderline irrelevant to the immediate discussion.

In almost any head to head matchup, the more captivating storyteller will run circles around the more proficient practitioner. The more potent bluff will make the more solid deliverable wholly invisible. The more dazzling magician will blot out the master craftsman through sheer force of theatre.

You can lament this as much as you like. You can say it rewards snake oil over honest toil, gloss over grit, memes over molecular facts. But the market doesn't care about your high-minded analysis. It's too busy throwing money at the most beguiling Emperors with the most ornate New Clothes.

So you have a choice as an entrepreneur. You can put your head down, build the objectively best mousetrap you can, and hope the masses smarten up. Or you can learn to play the bluff better than the next chump while still delivering something you can stand behind.

Anti-Bum Shield

But you can't pretend the game isn't the game just because you find it distasteful.

When all is said and done, people vote with their wallets. And those votes go to whoever can inspire the most belief in the minds of customers with the most cultural sway. Not the one with the cleanest code, the most defensible IP, or the best built gizmo. He who frames the value equation with the most audacity and conviction, sells.

Does that mean there's no room for ethics or integrity in your bluffs? Of course not. The best hustlers know being crooked is the fastest way to get got. You still want to deliver something of actual worth at the end of the day, lest you become just another cautionary tale.

But what you're really delivering is a FEELING. An experience of your prospects' puffed up self-image concentrated into a tangible expression. A tiny hit of the kind of importance and in-group recognition we're all secretly pining for. You can get there through your feature set and unique value prop. But not if it's not wrapped in the right mythology.

So study the greatest bluffs in your industry. Reverse engineer why they land with such force in the collective psyche. See if you can spot the gaps between objective reality and cultivated perception. Deconstruct the carefully crafted lore that elevates them from also-ran to top of mind and tip of tongue.

Then get to work on your own Bluff 2.0. Figure out the grandest claims you can make with a straight face given your positioning. Uncover the most fiendish angles you can take to reframe the game in your favor. Tap into the zeitgeist and locate your offering as the inevitable answer to the public's most pressing prayers, spoken or not.

Do it artfully, ethically, and with a product that actually puts in work to back up your most outlandish assertions. Execute with unshakable conviction and watch how quickly the usual sticking points melt before your bluff-fueled bravado.

The bluff doesn't just wag the dog in business. It is the whole damn kennel. So get out there and start spinning some tall tales around your humble value props. Speak them into being with the confidence of a carnival barker crossed with a megachurch preacher. And prepare to be amazed as your pretty little fictions turn the most jaded skeptics into FOMO-crazed fanatics.

Your numbers will never lie even if your marketing material waffles between diplomatic and delusional. All that matters is the scorecard at the end and how well you bluff your way into the hearts and minds of the right marks. The rest is just the cost of doing business in a world gone mad for self-serving narratives.

Key Ideas of Chapter Eight

1. Mastering the art of storytelling and perception management is crucial to business success.

2. Pricing power comes from the narratives and status associations you create, not objective measures.

3. Manufactured scarcity and exclusivity can dramatically elevate the allure of your offerings.

4. Skillful bluffing, or persuading others of the value of something, is a common tactic in achieving business success.

5. Back up bold claims with real substance, but lead with the most captivating stories.

Questions for self-development

- Am I too focused on objective measures vs. the perceptions and narratives I'm creating?

- How can I ethically leverage scarcity and exclusivity to boost my brand's magnetism?

Anti-Bum Shield

- What are the most potent status associations and self-images my prospects want to buy into?

- Have I been timid in my messaging when I should be making bolder, more audacious claims?

- Reflecting on the concept of money as faith expressed in numbers, how does this change my perspective on pricing, value creation, and marketing strategies?

- Can I identify instances where I've been swayed by the bluff in a business context? How does recognizing this influence my future decision-making?

- What new "bluff" could I introduce to radically reframe my market and tilt the game in my favor?

Chapter 9: How to create belief that what you offer is worth a lot?

Anti-Bum Shield

If you want to command top dollar for your products or services, you need to master the art of making people BELIEVE your stuff is worth the price tag. And that all comes down to understanding how your target audience perceives and measures value. Nail that, and you can pretty much write your own checks.

See, humans are funny creatures. We like to think we make decisions based on cold hard facts and logic. But the truth is, our beliefs about what something is worth are shaped by a million little subconscious cues and associations. Colors, words, images, context - they all come together to create a gut feeling about the value of an offering. Your job is to orchestrate those details into a symphony that screams "premium" at every touchpoint.

Take luxury watches for example. You can have two timepieces with pretty much identical specs and functionality. But slap one in a velvet-lined mahogany box with some flowering prose about "horological heritage" and "timeless craftsmanship", and suddenly it's worth 50X the other. The actual object didn't change one iota. But the STORY you spun around it jacked the perceived value through the roof.

Same goes for personal services. If you're a trainer trying to attract high end clients, you can't just rely on your technical chops and program design. You need to cultivate an aura of exclusivity and insider access. Focus on building a reputation as the go-to coach for celebs, athletes, and media stars. Pepper your marketing with name drops and co-signs from heavy hitters in your space. Make it clear that training with you puts people in a rarefied group that normals can't touch.

That's the beauty of the belief game. You don't need to have the fanciest facility, the most alphabet soup after your name, or the slickest sales pitch. You just need to create the IMPRESSION that your time and attention are scarce resources reserved for the select few. Whom you associate with, how you carry yourself, what you post on the 'gram - it all feeds the narrative that if someone wants a piece, they better get in line and open their wallets.

Of course, the catch is you can't just PRETEND your way to premium prices. There has to be some substance behind the sizzle. If you're dropping jaws with your client list and positioning, you better be ready to back it up with a truly standout experience. The quickest way to puncture your own hype balloon is to attract Grade A players then give them Grade C service.

Anti-Bum Shield

But when you match world class basic with the right world class packaging, you hit the believe jackpot. Suddenly, price becomes an afterthought. Your creme de la creme clientele will practically throw money at you for the privilege of basking in your reflected glory. They're buying a feeling, an identity, a story they can tell themselves and others about who they are and where they belong. And that intangible "it factor" is worth more than any perk or benefit you can list on paper.

So how do you get there? How do you imbue your offerings with the kind of mythical value that makes people scramble to give you their hard-earned cash? Honestly, a lot of it comes down to sheer audacity. You have to BELIEVE in your bones that your stuff is priceless. That your time is worth its weight in gold. That access to your world is a rare privilege that few will ever experience.

When you emanate that unshakable conviction, people can't help but buy in. They look at the way you move, the company you keep, the opportunities you casually mention, and think "damn, this cat must be the truth." That's when the real magic happens. Your unwavering belief in yourself transfers to them by osmosis. They start to see you through the same rose-colored lens you've worked so hard to craft.

But here's the tricky part: you can't just flip that belief switch at will. It's not about putting on an act or parroting some incantations in the mirror. People can smell a fraud a mile away, especially at the highest levels. No, to TRULY emanate that "it factor" energy, you need to dig deep and do the inner work. Examine your doubts and insecurities. Ruthlessly eradicate any hint of impostor syndrome. Surround yourself with people and experiences that reinforce your vision of how the world should see you.

It takes time, effort, and a whole lot of intestinal fortitude. But slowly, surely, you'll start to BECOME the person that matches your premium positioning. That unflappable confidence and quiet power will seep into your every move. And when your inner belief aligns with your outer packaging, clients won't stand a chance. They'll be tripping over themselves to give you whatever it takes to join your world and soak up your rare essence.

So take a hard look at your current offer and ask: does every detail scream "1 of 1?" Does my presence and poise shatter expectations of what this industry is about? Do I carry myself like someone who should be talking to the top 0.001% - and have the chops and connections to back it up?

If not, it's time to level up. Tighten your backstory. Upgrade your associations and appearances. Cultivate that "touch of inaccessibility" that makes people crave your attention like a drug. And most importantly, do whatever it takes to feel in your guts that you DESERVE to command a king's ransom just for being you.

Again, the hardest part is being ready to process it correctly. Let's imagine millionaire walks in there right now. We'll do some super wet fantasies. And he's like, "Well, what's up, guys". And you're like, "Come on, I want to train you." You say - "I want to train you." Millionaire - "Oh, yeah, fuck, let's start tomorrow. How much does your staff cost?" Pause... . So, my original invention, to sell, you have to feel entitled. And how do you make yourself entitled?

Key Ideas of Chapter Nine

1. Orchestrate every detail of your marketing to signal premium value and status.

2. Build a reputation as the go-to provider for a high-powered, insider clientele.

3. Create the impression that access to you is a scarce and coveted resource.

4. Back up bold positioning with an truly exceptional customer experience.

5. Develop rock-solid belief in your own value and right to premium prices.

Questions for self-development

- How can I infuse every touchpoint with cues that scream "high-end" and "exclusive"?

- What name drops, co-signs or associations would skyrocket my perceived status?

- Am I doing enough to create an air of scarcity and insider access around my brand?

- Does my actual delivery live up to the premium expectations I'm setting?

- How can I cultivate unshakable inner conviction and quietly powerful poise?

- If my self-image matched my premium positioning, how would I show up differently?

- Am I fully prepared to seize opportunities that come my way? How can I improve my readiness to take advantage of these moments to enhance my value proposition?

Chapter 10: To Sell, You Must Feel Entitled

Anti-Bum Shield

To make real money in business, you must cultivate a genuine, deep-seated belief that what you're offering is worth every penny you're charging – and then some. Lacking this unshakable conviction in your own value will leave you perpetually struggling to ask for the prices you deserve.

I've seen this issue trip up so many talented entrepreneurs and service providers. They have incredible skills, knowledge, and ability to get results for their clients. But when it comes time to put a price tag on their work, they balk. They feel weird, uncomfortable, even guilty about charging premium rates. So they lowball themselves, overdeliver like crazy, and end up resentful and burned out.

My friend Vadim is a perfect example. This dude is an absolute beast in his field - training elite athletes and getting them into the best shape of their lives. By any objective measure, he should be commanding obscene prices and have clients beating down his door.

But you know what? Vadim still undercharges massively relative to the insane value he provides. And it's not because he lacks the chops or reputation to justify premium fees. It's because deep down, he doesn't believe he DESERVES to be highly compensated for his work. In his mind, only sleazebags and scammers make the big bucks - not honest, hardworking guys like him.

It's a classic case of impostor syndrome mixed with money mindset issues. And it's costing Vadim a fortune in both income and impact. By refusing to claim his worth, he's not only leaving piles of cash on the table - he's limiting the number of people he can help with his amazing gifts. All because he can't wrap his head around the idea that he's entitled to be richly rewarded for the incredible value he provides.

Now contrast that with my own story. By most conventional measures, I shouldn't be nearly as successful as I am. I'm a total novice in my field, a college dropout with no fancy degrees. I started out figuring everything out as I went along, making it up on the fly. And yet, I've managed to build an audience of over 11,000 subscribers and create multiple thriving income streams.

Why is that? How is it possible that a "nobody" like me is kicking so much ass while a world-class talent like Vadim struggles? Is it because I'm smarter, more skilled, better educated? Hell no! Vadim has me beat by a country mile in all those departments.

The key difference is that I've cultivated an unshakable BELIEF in the value of what I offer, and my right to be highly compensated for it. I know in my bones that the insights and strategies I share are game-changers for the right people - and I'm not afraid to put a premium price tag on that transformation.

But here's the thing: that rock-solid conviction didn't come overnight. Like most entrepreneurs, I struggled hard with impostor syndrome and money hang-ups when I first started out. I would look at other experts charging top dollar and think "Who am I to ask for those kinds of rates? I'm nowhere near as qualified or experienced as they are!"

It took a lot of deep inner work (and some real talk from mentors) for me to realize that my worth as a teacher has NOTHING to do with my credentials or years in the game. My value comes from the RESULTS I help people achieve - the breakthroughs, the "aha" moments, the radical shifts in their lives and businesses.

Once I really GOT that, everything changed. I started showing up to sales conversations with a completely different energy - not tentative or apologetic, but calm and confident in the ROI I provide. I stopped stressing about prospects who scoffed at my rates, and focused on finding the PERFECT fits who were thrilled to invest at my level. And my income and impact started to skyrocket accordingly.

But it all started with that mental shift around my own sense of entitlement. I had to retrain my brain to accept that I was WORTHY of premium prices - that my work DESERVED to be richly compensated, no matter what any naysayers or haters had to say about it. I had to learn to value my own genius and results SEPARATE from outside validation or permission.

A big part of that was getting crystal clear on the unique GIFTS I bring to the table, and the specific transformations I facilitate for my clients. Instead of downplaying my skills with thoughts like "Eh, I'm not that special, there are way more qualified people teaching this stuff," I began to OWN my zone of genius.

I would highlight the RESULTS my clients were getting and say things like:

Anti-Bum Shield

"Sure, this information might seem super basic to a grizzled pro like me. But for the millions of people who have NEVER been exposed to these fundamentals of health and performance? It's an absolute game-changer, a quantum leap forward. And while other experts make it overly complex, I have a knack for explaining it in a way that is simple, clear, and crazy-effective to implement. That's the gap I'm filling and the value I provide."

See how that works? Instead of fixating on my "shortcomings," I focused on the tangible, needle-moving OUTCOMES my teaching style enables - and the massive NEED it serves in the market. Then I anchored my prices to that value.

This mental jujitsu is so key for anyone who wants to charge premium rates. You have to train your brain to believe on a gut level that your methodology is WORTH the investment you're asking people to make - and then some. You need an unshakable internal CONVICTION that your work deserves to be well compensated, based on the transformations you deliver.

And that conviction has to be so strong, SO deeply internalized, that no amount of impostor syndrome or outside resistance can threaten it. Because trust me, if you're doing it right, there WILL be skeptics and haters galore - that's just the price of entry for playing a big game.

But when YOU know your value, it won't matter. You'll be able to FEEL in your bones that you're meant to prosper. You'll show up to sales situations not from a place of neediness or anxiety, but from a calm inner POWER that magnetizes perfect-fit clients.

To cultivate that, you have to get radically honest about the TRUE worth of what you provide - not what you think you "should" charge based on your experience level, but what feels genuinely GOOD to your soul. And the more you live from that place of unshakable value, the more unstoppable you become.

Now, this mental shift takes WORK. Our culture loves to peddle the toxic myth that we're only "allowed" to charge big money if we have fancy credentials or decades of experience - as if a degree determines the value you can create for your market!

Anti-Bum Shield

But that's complete bullshit. Just look at all the paper-degreed, conventionally "qualified" experts struggling to make ends meet, while college dropouts and unlikely heroes CRUSH it in business simply because they've claimed a bold vision and learned to communicate their value.

At the end of the day, your earning power has NOTHING to do with your background or resume. It's about your ability to hone in on a burning NEED in your market, develop a unique solution, and then SELL that solution by speaking to your people's deepest desires and beliefs.

Do you think the market cares whether you learned your craft at Harvard or in the school of hard knocks? Fuck no! The market is ruthlessly results-oriented. If you can reliably solve a hair-on-fire problem or unlock life-changing results, clients will HAPPILY pay you top dollar regardless of your "on paper" qualifications.

The first step is deprogramming yourself of the belief that you need some external stamp of approval to merit premium prices. That you're somehow "less than" the gurus and need to grovel for scraps until you measure up to their stature. What a crock of shit!

Here's the damn truth: NOBODY is going to give you permission to charge what you're worth. No gatekeeper is going to show up and validate your value in the marketplace. That's on YOU, boo. It's YOUR job to claim your lane, OWN your genius, and then charge accordingly without apology.

So how do you do that, exactly? You start by getting ANGRY. Angry at a system that profits from your smallness. Angry at the societal programming that taught you to downplay your own brilliance. Angry at ANYTHING that stands between you and the prosperity you deserve. Anger is FUEL - so burn, baby, burn.

Then you get HUNGRY. Ravenously hungry for growth, for expansion, for MORE. More impact, more influence, more income, more of EVERYTHING you desire. You cultivate an unquenchable thirst for leveling up your skills and value so you can serve your people on the highest possible level. And you let that hunger drive you to do the uncomfortable things success demands.

Anti-Bum Shield

Finally, you go ALL IN on your market. You become a ferocious scholar of their deepest pain points, needs, and desired outcomes. You learn the specific language they use to describe their struggles and map out their wildest dreams. You crack the code on their buying psychology so you know EXACTLY what moves them to invest.

And then you create an offer that speaks to their needs so powerfully, so magnetically, that the value becomes undeniable - regardless of price point. You sell them what they WANT in a way that gives them what they NEED. And you do it so well, they almost have to talk themselves OUT of working with you!

That's when the real magic starts to happen. When you become so obsessed with SERVING your market that your self-image shifts. You're no longer some fraud just counting the days until you "make it." You're the real fucking deal, and you KNOW it. And so do your clients.

You start EMBODYING your value. Your income becomes simply an outer reflection of your inner sense of worth. And you show up to EVERY sales interaction absolutely certain the other person would be damn lucky to work with you - no convincing or coercion necessary.

Does this mean you never experience doubt or fear again? Fuck no. We're human. Even the highest earners still feel impostor syndrome nipping at their heels from time to time. The difference is that they've developed the mental MUSCLE to alchemize those doubts into fuel for even bolder action.

At the end of the day, the ability to claim your worth is like any other skill. It takes practice, patience, and a willingness to push past resistance. You have to CHOOSE to value your gifts in the face of all opposition. You have to DECIDE you're the shit and then back that up with massive action. No one can do that for you.

But the more you flex that muscle, the more AUTOMATIC it becomes. The more easily you show up to sales conversations utterly grounded in your worth. The more INEVITABLE your success becomes, because you're finally an energetic match for the money you want to make.

Anti-Bum Shield

Let me put it this way: the world is absolutely STARVING for what you have to offer, whether you see it yet or not. There are more opportunities, more abundance, more cash just waiting to throw itself at you than you can possibly fathom. But it can't reach you until YOU make the internal shift required to magnetize it.

Your earning potential is not determined by your credentials or years of experience. It's determined by the DEPTH of your connection to the value you provide and the FEROCITY with which you're willing to claim that value in the marketplace. End of story.

No one is coming to tap you with a magic wand of worthiness. No one is going to roll out the red carpet to your success. But those who DECIDE to prosper, do. Those who decide their work is worth top dollar, GET top dollar. It really is that simple.

Key Ideas of Chapter Ten

1. Your income is a direct reflection of your own sense of worth and value, not external factors.

2. To earn premium prices, develop unshakable belief in the results and transformations you enable.

3. Impostor syndrome and money blocks are the biggest obstacles to charging what you deserve.

4. Get intimately attuned to your market's deepest pain points, desires and buying psychology.

5. Mastering your inner game around value is the key to unlocking your full earning potential.

Questions for self-development

- Do I have unwavering conviction in the worth of what I provide, or do I harbor hidden doubts?

- Am I basing my prices on the massive results I get for clients or on irrelevant external measures?

- How can I cultivate rock-solid inner belief in my value and right to premium compensation?

Anti-Bum Shield

- What are the unique gifts and needle-moving outcomes that set my work apart in the market?

- Where am I still looking for outside permission or approval to charge high-end rates?

- Am I more obsessed with serving my audience powerfully or protecting my inadequacy stories?

- What internal shifts do I need to make to magnetize the income and impact I desire?

- If I already saw myself as a top-dollar expert, how would I show up differently in my business?

Chapter 11: Might is Right

Anti-Bum Shield

In the ruthless arena of business, there's a hard truth most people shy away from: Might is right. Power is right. If you can find a way to get the masses to throw millions at you for something as seemingly trivial as cheap keychains, then you have every right to do it and reap the spoils.

Now, some might object - "But what about providing real value and benefit to people? Isn't that what business should be about?" And sure, in a perfect world, that would be lovely. But we don't live in a perfect world. We live in a world where the market decides what has value, not some lofty moral code.

It's like watching a fight where a rough, unpolished brawler somehow manages to take down a more technically skilled, refined opponent. It doesn't compute on paper - the trained fighter should come out on top every time. But in the heat of battle, when fists are flying and adrenaline is pumping, sometimes raw power and aggression can overwhelm technique and finesse.

Look at a beast like Francis Ngannou in the octagon. The man is a hulking mass of muscle and fury who seems to defy the laws of physics with his punching power. His style may be a bit wild and unrefined compared to more classically schooled fighters. But you know what? He gets results. He knocks people the fuck out. He wins fights. And at the end of the day, that's what matters.

The same principle holds true in business. You can have the most polished, perfect product or service in the world, but if you don't know how to sell it, if you can't get people to actually buy - you're dead in the water. Meanwhile, the guy with the half-baked idea and the killer instinct for closing deals will be laughing all the way to the bank.

Now, does this mean you should completely disregard the notion of providing value and benefit to your customers? Of course not. That's a surefire recipe for eventual failure and a tarnished reputation. But it does mean that your ability to impose your will on the market, to generate serious demand and desire for what you're offering, is just as critical (if not more so) than the inherent quality of your product itself.

Think about it in terms of raw cost-benefit: If you're a highly skilled neonatologist working yourself to the bone saving premature babies in the ICU, you're providing immense, almost immeasurable benefit to society. You're literally saving lives, giving fragile little humans a fighting chance at a future.

Anti-Bum Shield

But if you're only earning 30-35k rubles a month for that invaluable service, while some Instagram influencer is raking in millions shilling diet tea and teeth whiteners...does that seem fair or right to you? Of course it fucking doesn't. But that's the cold reality of the marketplace. It's not about what should be valuable based on some moral calculus. It's about what the masses are actually willing to pay for.

So how do you cultivate that ability to shape the market to your will and start commanding the income and respect you deserve? In my experience, it all comes down to your capacity to sell. To persuade. To imbue your offer with so much perceived value that people would be fucking crazy not to take you up on it.

Because here's the thing - most folks have a serious aversion to selling. They think it's icky, manipulative, beneath them somehow. They labor under the delusion that if their product or service is just good enough, it should sell itself. But that's a fatal fallacy. Even the most objectively brilliant, groundbreaking ideas and inventions in the world won't make a dime without someone actively championing them and convincing others of their merit.

The truth is, if you want to thrive in business (and in life), you need to get cozy with wielding your power. You have to develop the capacity to impose your will on the world, to bend reality to your vision. You have to be willing to unapologetically convince others of your immense value and persuade them to pony up what you're worth, whether that's for a product, a service, or even just an idea.

Now, this doesn't mean you have to turn into some kind of soulless, Machiavellian psychopath. You don't need to manipulate or deceive anyone. But you do need to cultivate the backbone to stand firm in your value, even (especially) in the face of skepticism or pushback.

You have to be willing to look a prospect dead in the eye and confidently declare, "This is my price. This is the tremendous value I bring to the table. And if you can't see that, no worries - there are plenty of others who will happily snap up this opportunity." You have to develop the resolve to walk the fuck away from lowball offers and energy-vampire clients who want to nickel and dime you, knowing in your bones that the right people will show up and joyfully invest in you.

Anti-Bum Shield

Because straight up, if you don't unwaveringly believe in your own value and capacity to transform lives/businesses, why in the hell would anyone else? If you're not willing to go to the mat for your worth, to demand the compensation and treatment you deserve, you'll forever be at the mercy of a marketplace that will bleed you dry and leave you for dead.

But when you can root down into your power, when you cultivate the conviction to stand firm in your value and hold the line on your prices and boundaries, that's when the real magic starts to happen. That's when you begin magnetizing the caliber of clients, the game-changing opportunities, the lucrative income streams that most people only dream about.

It's not about being the most technically skilled, the most highly credentialed, the most "gifted" by conventional standards (although those things can certainly help). Nope. It's about developing the intestinal fortitude to back yourself fully. It's about being the most audacious, the most convincing, the most magnetic mofo in your space. It's about radiating an energy of quiet, unshakable confidence so compelling, people can't help but be drawn into your orbit.

When you can rock that, when you can fully own your inherent power and value and make it irresistible to your market, you've got a license to print money, my friend. And it doesn't matter if you're hawking fucking keychains or high-end consulting services - if you can get people believe in what you're selling, if you can generate an avalanche of desire, the sky's the fucking limit.

But it starts with reclaiming your own sense of entitlement. With deprogramming all the toxic bullshit society has force-fed you about being meek and mild and never rocking the boat. With giving yourself permission to be brazenly, defiantly powerful in pursuit of the prosperity and impact you were put on this earth to create.

So if you're done settling for table scraps and pity payouts in your business, it's time to step the fuck up and own your might. It's time to stop hiding your light and start imposing your will and your vision and your value on a market (and a world) in desperate need of what you have to offer.

Will it be easy? Fuck no. Claiming your power and charging your worth never is, especially if you've been conditioned to undervalue yourself for a long time.

Anti-Bum Shield

But is the the alternative of staying stuck in scarcity and resentment and soul-sucking "just getting by" better? I think we both know the answer to that.

You have gifts the world needs. You have problems you can solve like nobody's business. Transformations you can facilitate that will be priceless to the right people. And you deserve to be compensated like a fucking king/queen for the results you create - not just in money, but in recognition, respect, impact.

So stop downplaying your magic. Stop settling for less than you're worth just to avoid ruffling some feathers. The world doesn't need another half-stepped, hiding-in-the-shadows entrepreneur. It needs you, in your full power and purpose and swagger. It needs your conviction and your courage and your unfuckwithable commitment to playing all out.

It's time to rise. To unapologetically claim the prosperity and prestige you know you're capable of calling in. To allow the wealth and success you've been fighting for to fucking flood into your reality. This is your game. Your empire. Your legacy to unleash.

So strap on your big kid britches. Roll up your damn sleeves. And let's do this thing, shall we? Your market is waiting. Your fortune is waiting. And the impact you're destined to make is ready to be unleashed. All you gotta do is say yes and seize it.

Yes, this will push you out of your cozy little comfort zone (and then some). It will stretch you to your edges and make you face down the parts of you that want to stay small and safe. But on the other side of that fire is freedom like you've never tasted. Power like you've never wielded. A life rich in every sense of the word.

And if not now, then when? If not you, then who? No more excuses. No more "I'm not ready." No more "Who am I to..." bullshit. The world needs your unapologetic shine like never before. And it's time to deliver, to answer the call your soul came here to fulfill.

I know you've got the guts. I know you've got the grit. Now it's time to couple that with the audacity, the swagger, the willingness to get in the fucking arena of your greatness and fight for the success you deserve.

Key Ideas of Chapter Eleven

1. The principle that power and the ability to convince others of the value of your offering are paramount in business.

2. Persuasion ability and boldly claiming your worth matter more than credentials.

3. You must overcome resistance to selling and assertively champion your value.

4. Truly believing in your worth helps you attract high-caliber clients and lucrative income.

5. Harnessing might with integrity is key to inevitable success and fulfillment.

Questions for self-development

- Where am I still downplaying my value or avoiding selling due to limiting beliefs?

- How can I cultivate the backbone to stand unwaveringly firm in my worth?

- What would change if I fully gave myself permission to powerfully claim my desires?

- Am I willing to walk away from lowball offers, knowing my ideal clients will show up?

- How can I radiate the quiet, magnetic confidence that draws success to me?

- What bold action am I being called to take to seize my greatness and make my impact?

- Where do I need to stop hiding and start imposing my will, vision and value on the world?

Chapter 12: The Two Types of Problems

People will pay you handsomely to solve two main types of problems in the business world. However, there's a catch — most folks don't even know what their REAL problems are. They often believe they've got it all figured out, but in reality, they're usually fixating on surface-level symptoms while ignoring the deeper root causes.

Take the example of someone who comes to you complaining about visible veins on their legs. They're self-conscious about how it looks and want a quick fix to get rid of them. Now, if you're like most providers, you might be tempted to just take that concern at face value and offer some superficial solutions - creams, compression socks, maybe a referral for laser treatments.

And sure, those Band-Aids might provide a bit of temporary relief or cosmetic improvement. But here's the thing - those bulging veins are likely just a SYMPTOM of a much bigger underlying issue. Maybe it's poor circulation from a sedentary lifestyle or junky diet. Maybe it's a genetic predisposition no amount of topical treatments will fully resolve.

The point is, if you ONLY focus on zapping away the surface blemish, you're not really solving their core

Anti-Bum Shield

problem. You might make them feel a smidge better in the short term, but you're not delivering any lasting value or transformation. Even worse, you're missing a golden opportunity to set yourself apart from all the other skin-deep snake oil peddlers out there.

On the flip side, if you take the time to dig deeper and suss out the REAL root causes driving those symptoms, you can offer a far more comprehensive, valuable solution. You can educate them on the true triggers of their vein woes and co-create a holistic game plan to boost their circulation, nourish their body, and optimize their all-around health for the long haul.

And here's the beautiful part - when you're able to pull that off, when you can solve the SOURCE of their struggles instead of just slapping some concealer on the signs, people will eagerly pay you a king's ransom for your expertise and guidance. Because you didn't just mask their misery, you gave them a whole new lease on life.

But here's the rub - most folks are so hypnotized by their surface-level hassles, they don't even realize there's a more menacing monster lurking in the depths. They're convinced if they could just nix those nagging veins or shed that last stubborn 15 pounds or bank an extra thou a month, all their troubles would evaporate and they'd be tickled pink.

But as any seasoned problem-solver knows, that's just not how this rodeo works. The REAL issues, the ones that drive people to fork over fistfuls of cash - are rarely the obvious ones shouting from the sidelines. Nope, they're the deep-seated, often subconscious shitstorms that keep people stuck on the hamster wheel of hollow fixes while their TRUE potential stays forever out of reach.

And the dirty little secret is, most people couldn't even pinpoint those subterranean stressors if you put a gun to their head. They'll rattle off a laundry list of pesky annoyances and petty gripes, but they won't have the self-awareness or vocabulary to nail the core patterns and beliefs that are ACTUALLY running the shit show behind the scenes.

Take the example of a clothing store girl who shared a revealing insight. Her coworker was amazed that she was able to sell so much to pensioners, given the small pensions in Russia. But the girl had a completely different perspective. She realized that pensioners actually have significant savings squirreled away, often upwards of a million rubles hidden under their coats.

Anti-Bum Shield

They've been saving their whole lives but don't know where to spend it. And sooner or later, she reasoned, they'll likely get scammed and lose it all anyway. So why not let them enjoy dressing well in their golden years, something they couldn't do in the Soviet era?

This girl understood that clothes can bring immense joy and self-esteem, especially to those who have been deprived of such luxuries. She didn't get caught up in surface assumptions about pensioners being too poor to afford nice things. Instead, she dug deeper to uncover their true desires and pain points - the regret of never having nice clothes, the fear of losing their savings to scams, the yearning to feel good about their appearance in their twilight years. By tapping into those raw nerves, she was able to provide immense value and rake in the rubles, while her coworker was left in the dust.

As any seasoned problem-solver knows, the REAL issues that drive people to pay top dollar are rarely the obvious ones shouting from the sidelines. Nope, they're the deep-seated, often subconscious shitstorms that keep people stuck on the hamster wheel of hollow fixes while their TRUE potential stays forever out of reach.

That's where YOU shine, you brilliant beast. As a world-class problem-predictor and value-creator, it's your sacred duty to help people pinpoint and untangle their REAL blocks - even (especially) when they're blind to 'em. You gotta dawn your detective cap, your therapist specs, your mad scientist goggles and get to WORK unearthing the authentic aches that keep your peeps unfulfilled and underwhelmed.

Take the example of fitness coaching. On the surface, someone may come to you wanting to lose 15 pounds or run a faster mile. But if you're worth your salt, you'll know those are just symptoms of deeper desires - to feel confident, energetic and irresistible in their skin, to prove to themselves that they have the discipline to achieve a goal, to finally break free from the shame and self-loathing that's plagued them for years.

If you ONLY focus on giving them a meal plan and an exercise routine, you'll be just like every other generic trainer out there. But if you can tap into their REAL psychological drivers, reflate their trampled self-worth, and empower them to see themselves as the hero of their own transformation - not only will the pounds melt off, but they'll gain an unshakable new identity that enriches every domain of their life. And they'll pay you a queen's ransom for it.

Anti-Bum Shield

But let's be real - nailing THAT caliber of problem-solving prowess is about as easy as polishing a turd into a diamond. It takes a level of acumen, instinct, and give-a-fuck that the average bear frankly doesn't have. You gotta be able to taste the subtext, probe the tender spots, and call bullshit on people's safe little narratives in a way that both freaks 'em out and lights 'em up about FINALLY evolving.

And more than anything, it requires HUGE cajones to look your harshest critics dead in the eye and OWN your worth, even (especially) when they try to tear you to shreds. Like when I started posting fitness training ads on Avito at 16 years old, charging 500 rubles for a two-hour session. My buddy Dmitry, a European kickboxing champion, basically threatened to come beat my ass for having the audacity to charge for my expertise at that age.

You know what I told him? "You're damn right I'm charging 500 rubles. And if you don't think I've EARNED the right to ask that, you're welcome to come take a shot at me. But know this - I KNOW my fucking value. I've put in the blood, sweat and hustle to get to this level, and I'm not about to let ANYONE shame me out of owning it. You got a problem with that? Too fucking bad."

THAT is the level of conviction you need to cultivate as a master problem-solver and value-creator. You've got to develop an unassailable faith in your own genius, even in the face of haters, doubters and Negative Nancies galore. You've got to be so anchored in your ability to transform lives and deliver mind-blowing breakthroughs, literally NOTHING can shake your inner game.

And the way you get there is by doing the deep WORK - excavating your lingering insecurities and self-defeating stories until they lose their death grip on you. Battling your own demons down to the bone so YOU become the authority on slaying inner dragons. Field-testing your proprietary solutions until you KNOW, beyond a shadow of a motherfucking doubt, that your medicine is the most potent on the market.

Because when you're rock solid in your gifts and your grit, no two-bit troll or triggered critic will EVER succeed in rattling you. When you've walked through fire to heal your own holes, you'll gain X-ray vision for calling out other people's most clenched-cheek coping mechanisms. And when you marry that penetrating

Anti-Bum Shield

insight with an arsenal of alchemical techniques for transmuting people's worst wounds into their greatest weapons, you'll CRUSH the competition without breaking a sweat.

So let this be your new barometer of badassery - not how impressive your accolades are or how much clout you can collect, but how masterfully you can sniff out and smother the secret shackles keeping your dream clients shackled to their self-made Suck. How deftly you can disentangle surface stumbles from core collapses and craft unconventional solutions so potent, so personalized, it feels like an act of grand larceny NOT to invest on the spot.

And for Christ's sake, do NOT beat yourself up if you're not a savant at this ninja fuckery yet. Unwinding and rewiring people's most clenched-cheek complexes is a practice, not a perfect. It demands a fierce cocktail of courage, creativity, and radical responsibility most mere mortals just don't have the chops or the stones to stomach.

So if you're SERIOUS about being the kind of problem-annihilator and wealth-warrior who commands king-kong cashflow AND transforms lives like an archangel on ayahuasca, then hunker down and do the

DEEP work. Channel your inner Columbo and get fanatical about dissecting every "presenting problem" down to its primordial ooze.

Conduct human behavior autopsies on yourself, on everyone you meet, until sussing out unspoken sorrows becomes your native tongue. Develop an encyclopedia of common cries for help and the concealed cuts that fester beneath them. Court controversy and break taboos in pursuit of the truth behind the facade, the muck beneath the mask. And above all, GET BUSY transmuting those basement-level blocks into earth-shattering breakthroughs with every weapon in your superhero arsenal.

Not because it's comfy. Not because it's cool. But because THAT is the real measure of a master - the magnitude of your guts to go there and the caliber of your gifts to move mountains once you do. THAT is how you separate yourself from the snake-oil shills and build a business, a body of WORK, that endures and expands for GENERATIONS.

Key Ideas of Chapter Twelve

1. Look beyond surface-level symptoms to identify the root causes driving people's challenges.

2. Focus on providing comprehensive solutions that address core issues, not just band-aid fixes.

3. Develop the acumen to uncover the unspoken pain points and desires beneath people's narratives.

4. Cultivate an unshakable faith in your value and ability to transform lives, even in the face of critics.

5. Do your own deep inner work to heal your blind spots and become a true authority in your space.

6. Solving significant problems brings not only financial rewards but also a profound sense of fulfillment and purpose.

Questions for self-development

- Where am I still settling for providing superficial solutions vs. digging for the real root issues?

- How can I sharpen my instincts for sussing out the unspoken struggles driving surface problems?

- What limiting stories or insecurities do I need to heal to develop unshakable conviction in my value?

- Am I playing it safe or boldly naming the elephant in the room in my client conversations?

- How can I stress-test my solutions to ensure they create deep, lasting transformations?

- What would need to change for me to know beyond a doubt that my work delivers mind-blowing results?

- How can I make unearthing and solving the real, subterranean problems my zone of genius?

APPENDIX

Well done for reaching the conclusion of this book! Whether you have gone through each page or rushed to this final chapter, I want to recognize your dedication and commitment to self-improvement.

If you're seeing this message, it indicates that you've finished the book or decided to stop reading it. If you are in the second group, I want to inquire one last thing: what made you buy this book initially? After deciding to purchase this book, you probably looked over a summary of what it covers and the guidance it offers. The act of reading this paragraph implies that you believe in the wisdom offered by a wealthy individual.

In this material, my goal has been to assist you in gaining a deeper comprehension of the world we inhabit by providing insights from successful businessmen and millionaires who have mastered the intricacies of the financial industry. I have provided tangible instances, hands-on guidance, and stimulating queries aimed at questioning your beliefs and motivating you to act.

However, the real potential of this book is not in the text written here, but in how you decide to act upon it. The knowledge and tactics I have provided are only instruments; it is your responsibility to take them and apply them in your own life.

While you ponder your journey and shut the book, keep in mind that development and achievement are continuous processes. There will always be additional knowledge to acquire, more inquiries to pose, and more obstacles to conquer. The important thing is to keep a curious and receptive attitude, to look for new chances to develop, and to keep moving forward even when the road ahead is uncertain.

Whether you're infused with motivation and prepared to face the world, or you're still dealing with hesitations and uncertainties, understand that by investing in yourself and your future, you've made a crucial move. It is now your responsibility.

Thank you for including me in your journey. I trust that the information and recommendations provided in this book will help you in maneuvering through the dynamic and evolving realms of business and personal development.

NOTES

The purpose of the Notes section is to help you grasp the concepts, ideas, and examples discussed in the book. Here, you will discover additional details such as a glossary, a list of abbreviations, and explanations of names, brands, platforms, and historical references cited in the text.

I recommend thoroughly exploring these notes, as they offer important context and clarity that can assist in fully understanding and implementing the book's lessons. Whether you decide to read the notes all at once or use them for reference when going back to certain chapters, they are available to help you on your learning path.

Glossary of Terms:

- Bitcoin: A decentralized digital currency that operates on a peer-to-peer network without the need for intermediaries.

- NFTs (Non-Fungible Tokens): Unique digital assets that are verified on a blockchain, often representing items such as artwork, music, or collectibles.

- LARP (Live Action Role-Playing): A type of interactive game where participants physically portray characters in a fictional setting.

List of Abbreviations:

- ICU: Intensive Care Unit

- UFC: Ultimate Fighting Championship

Explanations of Names, Brands, and Platforms:

- Arsen Markaryan: An Armenian dollar millionaire and owner of a large private Telegram channel.

- Telegram: A cloud-based instant messaging and voice-over-IP service.

- Avito: A Russian online marketplace and classified advertisement website.

- Alfa Group: One of the largest privately owned investment groups in Russia.

- Lionel Messi: An Argentine professional footballer.

- Francis Ngannou: A Cameroonian mixed martial artist and professional boxer.

- Instagram: A social networking service for sharing photos and videos.

- Sergey Svetlakov: A Russian actor and comedian.

- Columbo: An American crime drama television series.

- Yahoo Finance: A media property providing financial news, data, and commentary.

Explanations of Companies and Brands:

- Ritz Carlton: A luxury hotel chain and subsidiary of Marriott International.

- Apple: An American multinational technology company known for consumer electronics and software.

- Fortune 500: An annual list of the 500 largest U.S. corporations by total revenue.

- Michelin-starred restaurant: A restaurant that has been awarded one or more stars by the Michelin Guide.

- Harvard: A private Ivy League research university in Cambridge, Massachusetts.

- Ferraris: Italian luxury sports cars manufactured by Ferrari.

- Nerf: A toy brand that produces foam-based weaponry and other toys.

- Benz: A German luxury automotive brand, short for Mercedes-Benz.

- Starbucks: An American multinational chain of coffeehouses and roastery reserves.

- BMW: A German multinational corporation that produces luxury vehicles and motorcycles.

- Cadillac: A division of General Motors that designs and builds luxury vehicles.

Historical References:

- Soviet era: The period when the Soviet Union existed, from 1922 to 1991.

www.ingramcontent.com/pod-product-compliance
Lightning Source LLC
Chambersburg PA
CBHW052204220526
45471CB00004B/1806